To Vic

KBP SMITH

MW00941234

# About the Book Cover

Sara Gettys' carvings — like the book cover's "Happy Day" — are inspired by the landscape and wildlife of Washington, from the sage of the Yakima Valley to the ferns and water of the Olympic Peninsula. Using spray paint and plants as "stencils," Sara works with form and color on a piece of plywood. She applies line and texture by cutting through the surface of the paint and the first layer of wood. Details are created with acrylic paint and other textural elements. The whole process involves working with layers — first in creating layers of form with natural materials and then revealing layers by carving through the surface of the wood.

# About the Artist

Sara Gettys is an artist and designer living in Olympia, Washington. She grew up in Oklahoma, attended college at Hollins University in Roanoke, Virginia, and then earned her master's degree in journalism at the University of Missouri. She was a photojournalist at the Yakima Herald-Republic for more than seven years before moving to Olympia to work for South Puget Sound Community College as a digital media producer.

# More To Crow About:
# Stories of Humor and Hope

# More To Crow About:
# Stories of Humor and Hope

**Spencer Hatton**

Copyright permission

Columns dated from January 30, 1994, through November 6, 2015, are reprinted by permission
of the Yakima Herald-Republic.

ISBN: 1514611953
EAN: 9781514611951

Hatton, Spencer. "More to Crow About: Stories of Humor and Hope." Self-published.
Printed by Createspace, Charleston, 2016. To order copies, go to www.SpencerHatton.com

*This book is dedicated to my son, Andy, and to my wife, Leslie, who have given me so much laughter, warmth and love, plus the all-important ingredient to life — hope.*

# Table of Contents

Cast of Characters

## Eat, Drink and then Drink Some More

## Memories

Afterword

# Foreword

Spencer Hatton is one of those people who is even funnier in person than in print, and he's plenty funny in print.

If you ever get stuck in a broken elevator, dangling from a threadbare chain for six hours, he's the one you'd want with you. Engaging, exuberant and droll, he can make a tense time seem fun. I know he did for me when I worked as a newspaper reporter under his editing tutelage for some 20 years. He was a wonderful and fun-loving, yet sensitive, boss and I think that joyous combination of mirth and goodness comes through in his writing.

Our jobs at the newspaper required a tough, demanding pace, but what I recall most is how many laughs we shared. That's Spencer. He comes alive in the following pages with wry observations on such delights as a vengeful stuffed turkey and a cat-enhanced steelhead marinade. He makes you smile, and he makes you think.

Sometimes comical, sometimes wistful, always trenchant, Spencer's commentaries will leave you hungry for more. Mostly he will leave you laughing, one of his great gifts.

Odd things have a way of happening to Spencer, but instead of grimacing, he records the experience, reminding us that not all days are going to be golden, like the time he planned what he thought would be a dream fishing trip with his wife, Leslie. First, they discover that what they had hoped was a four-star accommodation turned out to be grossly devoid of any celestial ratings, and instead was filled with a disturbing array of teddy bears. Next, even though they never see a fish, their fishing lines snap in unison. Finally, they find themselves eating dinner in the company of a one-legged accused killer.

Providing rueful commentaries on the things that matter most to us (and a few that don't), he doles out humor and wisdom with insightful precision. His reminiscences may be quirky and mirthful, but all are life affirming.

He has an all-encompassing enthusiasm for life. However, like life itself, not all of Spencer's subjects revolve around humor, such as when a dear friend dies and Spencer and Leslie take on the formidable task of cleaning out his yard, discovering that it had never been touched by pruners, saws or shovels before. Still, they persist and leave no stone unturned.

Spencer also pays homage to people who played important roles in his life, including a heartfelt appreciation for two remarkable teachers. They spring to life as he sets the scene, and it's not hard to imagine a scrawny fourth-grader (Spencer) playing the suave part of Fred Astaire to his beloved teacher in dance class. (You'll just have to read it.) As for his high school Latin – yes, it was that long ago – teacher, here's how Spencer's colorful description paints a character we won't forget:

> "To put it bluntly, Mr. Van Dyke was oddly shaped, like a large, over-ripened pear. His oval face was topped with black, thinning hair that roamed riotously over his pointed head. He wore thick, black-rimmed glasses that only helped accentuate his bulging eyes, which seemed ready to burst. His shirt refused to be tucked in, and his tie, always black and pencil-thin, hung crazily from his neck. Call him "disheveled" and you would be paying him a compliment."

For those of you who have waited with delicious anticipation for this, his second collection of newspaper and magazine columns, here's your reward. And for those who are reading Spencer for the first time, you're in for a lovely treat – and a wild ride.

Here, then, are Spencer's words, the fullest expression of a generous and gracious man. And what could be better than that?

— Jane Gargas

# The Lighter Side

*"From there to here, and here to there, funny
things are everywhere."*
— DR. SEUSS, FROM "ONE FISH, TWO
FISH, RED FISH, BLUE FISH"

# Never overpromise when taking a trip

*"The best laid plans of mice and men often go awry."*
— ROBERT BURNS

*August 12, 2012*

The dog days of summer usher in what has become for me a dreaded ritual — the August vacation. While others head out to the Oregon coast for brisk walks along the sandy shores of Cannon Beach, I prefer more pedestrian pursuits. Take, for instance, my trek last August to Lake Roosevelt with my wife, Leslie.

Despite detailed preparations, it turned into a bad reality TV show. I committed the No. 1 sin of vacation planning. I overpromised — guaranteeing fine dining and fantastic fishing.

While my late wife loved to camp along desolate stretches of Lake Roosevelt, Leslie's idea of roughing it is to reserve a corner room at a four-star hotel with fluffy bathrobes and 24-hour room service.

I figured I had to find just the right spot for her. I set my sights on Seven Bays, a summer resort area with a marina and several housing developments along the southeast shores of Lake Roosevelt, some 60 miles from Spokane.

But where to stay at Seven Bays? With no plush resorts in the vicinity, I sat down at the computer and typed in four letters that every vacation planner has memorized: VRBO (Vacation Rentals By Owner). In a minute I was scrolling through the amenities for a two-bedroom rental at Seven Bays. At $99 a night, it was a steal.

There was one hitch. It was a manufactured home. Would Leslie veto the rental? Though there was no mention of a bathrobe in the closet, Leslie lowered her standards. "OK, hit the buy button," she said, her voice tinged with a note of resignation.

Our arrival to Seven Bays began on a high note. A party of six deer welcomed us. Leslie shrieked with delight. Not a bad way to start the vacation, I thought to myself.

That, sadly, was the high point.

Stepping inside the manufactured home was like walking into a time portal from Star Trek. It reeked of the 1970s. The only thing missing was the disco ball spinning wildly in the living room. What it didn't lack were stuffed bears. They were everywhere.

Leslie holds up the only fish we caught on the trip.

Matters got worse the next day. Fishing proved challenging. We had more luck snagging the bottom of the lake than hooking a trout. During one of those snags, I somehow got the thin fishing line wrapped around my wristwatch. After uttering a string of curses, I turned off the motor. Not a good idea. Leslie's line also got stuck on the bottom. Both fishing lines then snapped in unison.

In the face of such adversity, Leslie decided to pose for a photograph. She held up a bag of Goldfish crackers. That proved to be the closest we ever got to a fish at Lake Roosevelt.

Still determined to salvage our vacation, I decided to take Leslie to dinner. We learned from the clerk at Seven Bays marina that the only decent place to eat in the area was the Fort Spokane Restaurant. "It has great prime rib on Friday," she exclaimed. I told her we were leaving on Thursday. She sighed and said, "Well, their hamburgers aren't bad."

That was good enough for me. After a short drive, we arrived at the restaurant, a dilapidated wooden building with a Bud Light logo in one window and a crude drawing of a bare-chested woman high above the entrance.

Inside we weaved our way down an aisle cluttered with bags of Doritos and canned Spam. We were met by a young man in his 20s, who greeted us with a smile and a story we found hard to follow and even harder to believe.

The young man said he was there with his older brother after a weeklong criminal trial. Apparently his brother had been involved in a terrible boating accident two years earlier on Lake Roosevelt. His brother and a friend were speeding along in a jet boat when they slammed into a huge rock. His brother was knocked unconscious and suffered busted ribs, punctured lungs and a crushed leg, which he eventually lost.

What happened to the other guy, I asked. He died, the young man said. That's why there had been a trial, he said. The county prosecutor wanted to convict his brother of causing the death of his boating companion. But his brother had no memory of the fatal crash and no one could determine who was driving the boat at the time of the accident, the young man said. That's why the jury set his brother free.

I felt like I was taking part in a therapy session, with the young man unburdening himself after weeks of anguish over his brother's tragic accident and the ensuing trial. I stared down at a canister of Pringles potato chips that I was clutching in my right hand. What am I doing here, I asked myself. I put the Pringles back on the shelf and patted the young man on the shoulder. A smile returned to his face.

Leslie and I found a table at the back of the restaurant, on the other side of a partition where the young man had rejoined his brother.

Though we sat alone at our table, we had company. Above us hung the outstretched wings of a wild turkey and, on a shelf along the wall, a Canadian goose and a cougar, whose glassy eyes peered down at us.

After a half hour, the waitress delivered our order. A trail of smoke rose up from the sizzled meat. I bit into my hamburger and nearly lost a tooth. It had been charred beyond recognition.

"That's him," Leslie whispered, grabbing my arm.

Who, I asked, wondering why her eyes had bulged to the size of Walla Walla onions.

"The older brother," she said.

Sure enough, there he was, skirting by our table in a tortured gait caused by his artificial leg.

"Great hamburgers," he hollered to the cook.

I gazed up at the gobbler, its long neck stretching out over my plate. A thin strand of cobweb, which had clung to its yellow bill, suddenly broke loose and floated down, landing in my french fries.

Some vacation, I muttered to myself. I can't even get a break from a stuffed turkey.

# The sex talk

**"L**et's talk about sex."

That's how my mother would open a conversation with my son, Andy, while he was growing up. You knew Mom was ready to breach the taboo subject when she would fidget about in her chair to get comfortable, one hand clutching onto a cocktail glass filled with crushed ice, vodka and an anchovy olive. A broad smile would sweep across her lips as she uttered the four words that would send Andy into a frantic retreat.

"No, Grammy, not the sex talk," he would exclaim.

It was innocent banter. The conversation would rarely go much further than the opening line.

And that's about as far as the sex talk got for me when I was also growing up.

"It's about time you learned about certain things," my mom told me one night after stepping into my bedroom. "Your Dad will be up to talk to you about sex."

So I positioned myself on the edge of the bed and waited, wondering how my Dad, an accomplished lawyer and gifted orator in the courtroom, would deal with the ticklish topic of the birds and the bees. I waited and waited. I stared at the clock. An hour passed. Soon I fell fast asleep.

Dad never did have the sex talk with me. I had to get the lurid details in the school locker room from a fellow classmate, Windy Holden, who offered his own colorful take on how babies are conceived.

Little did I know late last year when I published my first book, "Counting Crows: Stories of Love, Laughter and Loss," that Mom's sex talk would again echo through my life.

It began innocently enough. After holding a successful book-signing event at Yakima's Inklings Bookshop in mid-December, I learned from the store's owner, Susan Richmond, that "Counting Crows" had become the store's top-selling book. Then it struck me. My compilation of newspaper columns had outsold the scandalously erotic romance novel, "Fifty Shades of Grey," an international best seller written by British author E.L. James. Now that's something to crow about, I thought.

But the buzz didn't end there. Earlier this summer Inklings' Richmond also informed me "Counting Crows" had outpaced book sales for another best-selling writer, Susan Mallery. A romance novelist with more than 80 Harlequin and Silhouette novels to her credit, Mallery has sold more than 25 million copies worldwide. Each time she publishes a book — she turns out four or five a year — it immediately zooms to the top ranks of The New York Times best-seller list.

Why should we care about Susan Mallery? Because she once made her home in Yakima. How do I know this? Because my wife, Leslie, and I lived across the street from her.

Her real name is Susan Redmond. She moved here from the Seattle area so her husband could take a job running a company. He later became the Yakima Air Terminal manager.

I wondered what our neighbor was up to when nearly every day a Federal Express truck would park outside her front door. Only later did we find out she was a romance novelist with a golden resume.

"Susan Mallery is one of my favorites," wrote Debbie Macomber, another fabulously successful romance writer who — are you ready for this? — is a Yakima native. She's sold more than 170 million copies. Who would have guessed our Yakima Valley, so rich in apples and wine grapes, is also fertile ground for purveyors of steamy bedroom romps.

Susan and her husband moved out of our quiet cul-de-sac in 2010, returning to Seattle where she continues to populate the publishing world with her novels while also providing lively updates on her website and Facebook page.

So what makes these romance novels tick? Is it all about sex, as my late mother would, no doubt, have argued in favor of?

In search of an answer, I pulled from our bookshelf "Under Her Skin," a romance novel Susan wrote in 2008 and gave to my wife to read. It's about Lexi Titan, heiress to a vast fortune who falls for Cruz Rodriguez, a Texas playboy "with money, success, smoldering good looks." I absentmindedly opened the book to Page 220. Here's what I read:

> "She never felt so exposed and sexually connected at the same time. She was totally at his mercy, unable to control anything about the experience. Trust was required. So she should have been uncomfortable, but this was Cruz, and for reasons she couldn't explain, she trusted him completely. … Heat filled her. Heat and need. Her muscles tensed. She felt herself getting closer … to the moment when she would fly out of control."

What are the chances of flipping open a romance novel and landing smack dab in the middle of a sex scene? Apparently, very good.

Trust me Susan Mallery has sizzle in her prose. But she doesn't dwell on it for an eternity. On Page 221, some six paragraphs later, Lizi is talking about cooking spaghetti dinner for the "smoldering" Cruz. Yes, even in romance novels, the lusty main characters still have to eat.

I have to face the facts of life — "sex talk" sells. Sadly, it's a topic I avoided in "Counting Crows." Though I have lots of passion in my prose, it's nothing compared to the fixation on frolicking foreplay that romance novels bring to bear (or is that bare?).

However, within the 319 pages of my first book, "Counting Crows: Stories of Love, Laughter and Loss," I do have a passage that could steam up a pair of reading glasses. It's from my writer's journal and details a date with my late wife Bronnie. It was at a body painting party in 1974 — and yes, back then, those kinds of frivolous activities were fairly common on college campuses.

"Her head tilted as I talked to one of her roommates. Bronnie's moist breath swarmed like bees buzzing into my ear. Her lips, marble smooth and glistening with delight, tacked from cheek to chin to lower lip, sailing with the breezes, as my head pivoted, frolicking in the warmth. She kissed. I too."

Hey, that's not too bad. Maybe I have what professionals call "the chops" for romance writing. But can I sustain that for 300 pages? It's worth a try. I know one thing for sure. My mother would have approved, and you can't get a better endorsement than that.

# Menace terrorizes the city

---

*December 9, 2012*

A menace roams the streets of Yakima and no one seems to care.
Well, I do.
In late October and early November, I had repeated run-ins with my archenemy, and it was never a pretty sight … or sound. My wife, Leslie, and I were on a mission to remind people to vote in the presidential election. We knocked on the doors of nearly 400 homes, and each time we stepped out of our car, a chorus of yelps from these scrawny creatures assaulted our ears.

In Greek mythology, the fearsome beast was called Cerberus, a three-headed hound that guarded the gates to the Underworld. In Yakima, the canine comes in a much smaller package but delivers a similar wallop. It also goes by a different name — Chihuahua.

Now don't get me wrong. I'm sure there are a few well-mannered, friendly Chihuahuas living in Yakima. Sadly, I didn't meet any during our three weeks of doorbelling. And it's not as if we didn't survey a wide swath of the area. We knocked on front doors in the north near Chesterley Park, in the city's midsection around Franklin Park and in the south below Washington Avenue. Our crusade even took us into Union Gap.

And everywhere we went, it was the same scene repeated endlessly. A few seconds after I closed the car door, the yapping would begin. Often the sound was in stereo since Chihuahuas seem to come in pairs.

This ear-splitting noise is vastly disproportional to the size of a Chihuahua, which has the profile of a Bud Light beer can and protruding eyes ready to pop out of their sockets at any moment. With ears sticking out like miniature Frisbees, the bony-ribbed, oftentimes hairless Chihuahua is an animal to be pitied — if it weren't for its demonic yapping.

At one home, after Leslie had knocked on the front door and failed to get a response, I could hear a side door open and then close shut. From along the side of the house, out sprang a Chihuahua, howling in a hoarse, rasping voice. What little hair it had atop its head stood straight up, giving the odd appearance of a punk rocker. Realizing that the dog's territorial instincts border on paranoia, we beat a hasty retreat to our car as the crazed Chihuahua continued its rant.

One afternoon while doorbelling in a mobile home park along Washington Avenue, we came upon a hapless pet owner who had difficulty repelling the advances of her two Chihuahuas.

"I've got to get rid of these dogs," she lamented.

She looked to me for salvation. Trying to yell above the yapping dogs, I replied, "No thanks. We already have two cats. They're enough trouble." I didn't mention that one of our cats requires daily medication for irritable bowel syndrome. But compared to a fidgety Chihuahua, I'd take a feline with intestinal distress any day.

I have nothing against pets. I don't care if they are four-legged, bipeds, covered with scales or feathers, shed hair or hurl hairballs. I've comforted all of them at one stage in my life.

My first pet — I was 5 at the time — was a goldfish I won at the county fair by successfully landing a ping-pong ball into its pint-sized fishbowl. Two weeks later, the goldfish met an untimely death and, in a ceremony filled with pomp and a few awkward moments, my brother and I flushed it down our toilet.

Once, for reasons that still escape me, I purchased a pair of rats for my oldest son, Andy, who was in elementary school at the time. They were cute when they were small but soon grew to such proportions that Andy wouldn't get near them. So we ended up giving the rats away to a family that answered our newspaper advertisement. They drove up in a beat-up station wagon, its muffler bumping along the pavement and exhaust smoke filling the air. As the mother carried the caged rats to her car, my son whispered to me, "Dad, are they going to eat them for dinner?"

"Of course not," I replied in a not-so-confident voice that only heightened my son's fears.

Yes, such is the agony and ecstasy of owning pets. But really, given all of the wonderful creatures available in this universe, what's the point of a Chihuahua?

The breed's past is obscured in mystery. Sightings of a miniature, nearly hairless dog have shown up in records kept by Spanish conquistadores in the early 18th century and center on a region in Mexico later called — drum roll, please — Chihuahua.

In 1904 the American Kennel Club gave its seal of approval to the breed, noting they are "graceful, alert and swift-moving with a saucy expression." The saucy part is certainly right. In the AKC's popularity rankings last year, Chihuahuas came in No. 14, sandwiched between Doberman Pinschers and German Shorthaired Pointers. Described as having either a Deer or Apple head, the pint-sized pooches go by such endearing names as Teacup, Pocket Size and Tiny Toy.

I shouldn't, though, be so quick to judge a pet by its breed, even the shrieking Chihuahua.

I discovered this invaluable lesson a few weeks ago while taking part in Camp Prime Time's annual Leftover Turkey Trot at the Yakima Greenway. After finishing the three-mile walk, I headed to the parking lot at Sarg Hubbard Park and came face to snout with a Chihuahua. A most unusual thing happened next. No yapping. The apple-headed canine instead seemed to smile back at me.

A few yards away, a man opened his car door and in jumped the Chihuahua. Off the two went, with the hairless pooch perched atop the steering wheel. Now that's a sight to behold.

Is that legal? Then I remembered. It's a Chihuahua. Why shouldn't it drive a car? They already rule the streets of Yakima.

# Falling into the arms of the Virgin Mary

*May 1, 2015*

Art, like beauty, may be in the eyes of the beholder, but don't forget the feet. One wrong step and that art piece you are gazing at may end up costing you a fortune.

I learned this lesson the hard way last fall while traipsing through the famed National Gallery in London. Our small tour group of 25 hardy souls had arrived for a two-hour visit led by our guide, who had spent years studying the stunning pieces of art on display in England's renowned gallery.

Our first stop took us to a section devoted to Medieval and Early Renaissance, with pieces ranging in age from 1260 to 1440. We reached a large room and headed to a far corner. We gathered around Van Eyck's "The Arnolfini Portrait" (1434). It's derisively called by some "The Shotgun Wedding," and for good reason. The painting shows what many once believe was a wedding ceremony with a stiffly dressed groom and his bride revealing the unmistakable signs of an impending birth.

I was at the back of the tour group and wanted to get a better view of the bulging belly. So I nudged my way around the group's right flank. This line of attack put me between them and a wall holding several paintings. I figured this was the best way to approach the Van Eyck masterpiece.

Wrong.

I failed to notice that the National Gallery had cordoned off a safety zone between onlookers and the art pieces. This barrier consisted of a clear elastic cord looped through floor-mounted stanchions. The cord rose some 16 inches high, reaching a point just below my kneecap. I know this to be true because that's where the cord hit my leg when I ventured forward.

The laws of gravity then took control.

My leg buckled underneath me. I found myself in a free fall, my body pitching crazily toward the wall. Instinctively I extended my right arm to break my fall, heedless of the fact that priceless art lay in the way. Two portraits were clustered to one side. Titled "A Man and a Woman," they are presumably of a well-to-do husband and his wife, both painted with oil and tempera on oak by the renowned artist Robert Campin around 1435.

"The Virgin and Child Before a Firescreen."

An empty space of about four feet lay between those portraits and a more colorful painting of "The Virgin and Child Before a Firescreen." Completed by a follower of Robert Campin in roughly 1440, the painting on oak depicts the Mother of Heaven breastfeeding the baby Jesus.

Watching this entire scene unfold behind me was a museum guard. His eyes must have bulged to the size of Windsor Castle dinner plates when he caught sight of my outstretched hand heading directly toward the Virgin Mary's exposed breast. An international crisis seemed to be a nanosecond away.

Then fate intervened, in the form of Raquel. In her early 40s, Raquel was the youngest in our group and happily possessed quick responses and a strong grip. She saw me teetering on the brink of utter disaster and performed an act of selfless heroism — she snared my left arm, pivoting my body in such a way as to miss, by a matter of inches, "The Virgin and Child."

"Get behind the barrier," bellowed the museum guard.

I recoiled from the fall and stood upright, my right arm returning quickly to my side. Raquel breathed a sigh of relief. I tried to pretend if nothing had happened.

"Not again," muttered my wife, Leslie. She had seen it all.

"Sorry," I mumbled under my breath.

Sadly, receiving a stiff reprimand from a gallery guard happens far too often in my life. In the words of baseball icon Yogi Berra, the National Gallery incident was "déjà vu all over again." A few months earlier, while visiting Chicago and its world famous Art Institute, I had an eerily similar run-in with public art.

It unfolded innocently enough. Leslie and I were enjoying a delightful lunch on the patio of the gallery's Terzo Piano restaurant. We had a stunning view of Chicago's iconic skyline. I couldn't resist taking a photograph so I ventured out past the patio's eating area. Blocking my way was a weird-looking, low-slung white object that snaked along the floor. It was a pathetic barrier for it was easy to step around. I wonder what that's made of, I thought to myself. So I gave it a swift kick with my right foot.

Not a good move. Behind me a guard appeared, glowering at me. "Is this art," I asked incredulously. He nodded his head.

"Sorry," I mumbled under my breath. In the distance, I could see Leslie doubled over in fits of laughter.

Again, it's not really how sharp your eyesight is when gazing upon irreplaceable art. It does, though, have everything to do with those size 10 shoes you are wearing.

# Lilith Fair from a male perspective

*July 18, 2010*

I spotted her first as we peered over a wooden fence separating the public and paparazzi from a small gathering of rock stars. She was walking toward us, talking on a cell phone.

"Lance Armstrong's a bum," I yelled out.

Sheryl Crow didn't bat an eye and continued chatting on her phone until she reached the door of a gleaming motor home.

I had expected some kind of reaction from the Grammy-winning singer when hearing Armstrong's name, the cycling phenom and seven-time Tour de France champion who idiotically — in my humble opinion — broke off their engagement four years ago. He blamed it on the older Crow's biological clock ticking away and her over-eagerness to get married. What a bunch of malarkey. He just couldn't handle her talent and fame.

Then opportunity stared at me again.

Crow emerged from the motor home a few minutes later.

"I was just kidding," I called out, hoping this time an apology might do the trick.

Again, no such luck.

She waved to several other fans and headed down the hill, away from us and toward the main stage where she would appear, several hours later, rocking and rolling for a throng of 9,000 at the Lilith Fair at the Gorge Amphitheatre in George.

Let's face it. I'm a lousy rock fan. Maybe it's the Hawaiian shirt I was wearing. I thought it looked cool, but I soon realized only one or two other guys at the Gorge had opted for the Tommy Bahama look.

Actually, "one or two" described the entire male population. We were in a distinct minority and that was by design. Inspired by singer and songwriter Sarah McLachlan back in the 1990s, Lilith Fair was conceived as an antidote to the testosterone-driven rock concerts at the time and a way to celebrate the genius of women.

After 1999, Lilith went into dormancy, only to be resurrected this year by McLachlan and others. But the past is hard to replicate. Its summer swing through North America has had a few hiccups along the way, with a dozen concerts being canceled due to poor ticket sales.

Still, Lilith stuck to its return visit at the Gorge on July 3 after an 11-year hiatus and was eagerly welcomed by sun-worshipping fans, who perched on lawn chairs or sprawled out on blankets, rising to their feet whenever the show's headliners — Crow, McLachlan and Sugarland — would belt out a tune.

My wife, Leslie, and I decided to forgo the lawn-chair section. Instead, I took out what amounted to a small loan to purchase tickets in the reserved seating area. We were a mere 16 rows back from where R&B singer Erykah Badu, decked out in a floppy satin hat, declared early in the evening she was a "warrior princess." The crowd responded with a few thousand fist bumps.

And have no fear, we clearly got our money's worth — from drunken rock fans throwing up in the aisles to security guards hauling off several recalcitrant celebrants, all women, who seemed more intent on arguing their case for innocence than simply giving up and agreeing with the security guards that, yes, they really didn't have a reserved ticket after all. And what's a rock concert without the acrid smell of marijuana wafting in the air? We got that, too.

But before singer Colbie Caillat, one of the warm-up acts, got a chance to croon Fleetwood Mac's "Go Your Own Way" to the delight of the assembled 8,972 women and 28 guys (that's my calculation), my wife and I took in some exquisite people watching.

They came in all shapes and sizes, some sporting bright neon red-dyed hair and a few women taking the clothing-optional route and going topless.

Tattoos also dominated the fashion scene. By my estimate, some 95 percent of those attending the all-day soiree had some form of etching embedded in their skin.

It was reminiscent of 14 years ago when I first spent a day at the Gorge. I had promised to take my son Andy to a concert, of his choosing, for his 15th birthday. What a mistake that was. A word of advice to parents: Never give a teenage son the freedom of choice. It always leads to disastrous results.

Instead of picking a sedate Beach Boys reunion concert, my son selected Lollapalooza. For the uninitiated, of which I was one, this concert series brings together the hottest, loudest, most profane heavy metal and alternative rock bands of the day. Topping the list of headliners back then was none other than Metallica, a band that's synonymous with the phrase "permanent hearing loss."

After a day of dodging small cumulus clouds of marijuana (again, a key ingredient to any rock concert), nightfall finally arrived and Metallica cranked up one of its signature tunes, "Creeping Death." That's when my son informed me he was going down there, pointing to what had become a massive mosh pit of writhing bodies in front of the main stage.

It turns out the mosh pit was in the exact same spot where Leslie and I were sitting for the Lilith Fair. How weird is that.

But the Gorge is all about connecting the dots. So it didn't seem odd when, for her final song, Sheryl Crow decided to do a tribute to Led Zeppelin, the band credited with giving birth to heavy metal. It ended with the drummer kicking his set across the stage and the backup singers ripping off their bras.

See what you're missing, Lance. There's nothing like rock 'n' roll to set you free.

*FOOTNOTE: Not only is Lance Armstrong a bum as I once declared, but as it turns out he's also a liar and a cheat. In 2013 during an interview with Oprah Winfrey, he finally confessed to using drugs to win his seven Tour de France titles. Armstrong was later stripped of those titles and also got slapped with a lifetime ban from cycling.*

# Oh, crap, there goes the iPod

*July 26, 2009*

Now I know why earphones were created: to keep your iPod from taking a dunk in the toilet.

I found that out firsthand on a recent afternoon at the Yakima Family YMCA.

After changing into my exercise clothes in the locker room, I made a short side trip to a nearby restroom stall.

Here's where the plot thickens. My regular running shorts were dirty so I had to wear an older pair — with no pockets. The lack of pockets is crucial here because I decided to tuck my iPod into the elastic band of my shorts. Made sense to me. You know the saying: "Out of sight, out of mind."

While lifting up the toilet seat, I saw something flash in front of me.

I instinctively reached out for it, but the object slipped through my fingers. I did, however, catch hold of the earphone's thin green cord. It's lucky I did, for dangling in midair, only an inch or two above the pale blue water of the toilet, was my iPod.

It's at these extreme moments when you confront one of the great mysteries in life: What is it with toilets? Why are they like black holes in the universe where everything gets sucked down into their swirling vortex?

Maybe that's why I've had so many run-ins, or rather drop-ins, with toilets. I have kerplunked just about everything into these porcelain thrones. Pair of eyeglasses? Done that. A favorite childhood puppet? Did that at age 6, much to my chagrin.

The list goes on: toothbrushes, a contact lens case and an actual contact lens, car keys, nail clippers, countless bars of soap.

The nearness of the bathroom sink has a lot to do with these royal flushes. And toilets seem so innocent looking, don't they? Who's to blame for its sinister design?

It's not Sir Thomas Crapper. Many have tried to point an angry plunger in his direction, but they're all wet. Indeed, there was a Thomas Crapper who had a number of toilet patents to his credit, but he's not enshrined in the Water Closet Hall of Fame.

That distinction goes to 16th century author Sir John Harrington. He actually installed one of the first flushing prototypes in the palace of Queen Elizabeth I, his godmother. Sadly, the queen didn't use it. She complained it made too much noise.

I'm sure she would have developed flusher's elbow if she had owned a modern-day Neorest toilet. This luxury Japanese-made model costs up to $5,200 and features a warm air dryer, catalytic air deodorizer, heated seat, oscillating spray massage and a front-and-back aerated warm-water spray. Now that's going first class.

Though the Neorest may be a bit much (the warm-water spray frightens me), toilets seem to attract an inordinate number of inventors. Scores of U.S. patents have been taken out over the years in hopes of bettering the plight for those of us venturing into the WC. Even Yakima shares in the patent craze, with at least two on file — a sanitary toilet lift in 1992 and an elaborate volume-selective water closet flushing system in 1989.

So if the common folk are so fixated with toilets, what about celebrities?

Have no fear. They are just as fascinated as we are.

Guess what Madonna requests when she arrives at a hotel for a performance? A new toilet seat. Each night. R & B performer Mariah Carey also demands that a new toilet seat greet her whenever she settles in for the night at a five-star resort. She likewise insists that all of the bathroom faucets be replaced with gold ones. Nice touch.

As for cleaning toilets, that honor goes to Miley Cyrus, better known to her adoring fans as superstar Hannah Montana.

"I worked at this place called Sparkles Cleaning Service and I cleaned houses," Cyrus said in a 2008 interview with Us Weekly magazine. "I was, like, 11 ... I can scrub a toilet."

But can you "scrub out" an iPod that's been chucked into a loo?

I decided to do some further research — on the Internet. I typed in "iPod in toilet" into my trusty Google search engine and uncovered 3,430,000 hits that mention this particularly embarrassing mishap. One overly descriptive entry referred to such an occurrence as an "iTurd moment." Now there's a phrase not worth repeating.

At www.methodshop.com, visitors are greeted to a video of an iPod splashing into a toilet that, quite frankly, has seen cleaner days. Solutions offered at this site range from using an alcohol pad for a quick cleanup to placing the dripping iPod near a heater to dry out. Most readers, though, confess they have resigned themselves to the fact their iPod is a goner.

The website does offer this consoling comment: "At least you didn't put it in the washing machine."

Of course not. That's reserved for cell phones.

# Porcelain doll dealing for fun and — well, fun

*February 20, 2005*

W hat's not to like with the redhead.

She's a knockout, poetry without motion. Her hair teases the air, and cascades down in wavy curls upon her shoulders. Her lips, mere wisps, are tightly pressed, in a perpetual pose of someone whispering. And her eyes, glowing green in the light, penetrate the stillness between us. It's as if she never blinks.

Yes, she's a looker. But what's with that velvet handbag? It's embroidered with white doilies, the kind of stuff my grandmother would place on the arms of her couch.

And get a wide-angle shot of her hat. Pink feathers. Now that's a fashion statement. But flash me a greenback with Andrew Jackson's face on it — 20 bucks, that's the asking price — and she's yours. I'll even stuff her into a plastic bag.

It may be a brutal, heartless business, but such is the life of a doll seller. That's me, or at least that was the role I played at the 23rd Annual Doll, Toy and Teddy Bear Show in the bottom floor of the Salvation Army building on 16th Avenue in Yakima. Forty tables were set up, overflowing with porcelain dolls just like mine.

Besides the redhead, l had more than 30 dolls of various sizes and shapes, mostly decked out in Victorian attire. My cousin's wife, Candy, donated the dolls for my late wife's scholarship fund, which supports special education students at Central Washington University. A very nice donation, except for one troubling aspect — I had to sell them.

So several months ago, I asked for help from Star Allen, an expert who has her own porcelain doll studio in Yakima's West Valley. With a friend in tow, Star showed up at my house to survey my bevy of dolls. I greeted them at the door like one of those folks you see on the "Antiques Roadshow," my eyes bugged out with visions of million dollar dolls dancing in my head.

No such luck. My dolls were fakes, all copies of originals.

Star forced a smile and said, "You might get 20 for that one." She was pointing to the redhead. This wasn't the kind of bounty I was dreaming about.

Despite the grim assessment, I still showed up at the annual doll show after being invited by Marlene Sybouts, a very warm-hearted lady and an experienced doll collector. How could I resist?

Now, I know this may sound odd, but the event was great fun. It had little to do with the dolls and everything to do with the doll collectors.

What I found, besides hundreds and hundreds of impish-looking dolls, were energetic ladies who seemed not only fascinated with everyone else's collectibles but also with each other's welfare. It was like a big family reunion. Laughter mingled with inquiries about grandkids and worries over a friend's recent surgery.

And what would a doll show be without Pauline Hunter and her famed hamburger soup.

Pauline is the warmest, friendliest person you could ever meet, and an ambassador of goodwill for Yakima's Salvation Army, where she serves as its program coordinator. Pauline knows everyone, and has a gentle word and eager smile for each person she meets.

But this past weekend, something was amiss with her hamburger soup, which she dishes out at most Salvation Army events.

"It doesn't taste right," she confessed to me as she swallowed another helping of her signature soup, the recipe for which one of her friends lifted out of the Yakima Herald-Republic years ago. "I forgot something. You try it."

So I slurped and agreed it lacked a certain pizzazz. It's good, though, I replied, trying to perk her up.

Two hours later, I was in line for lunch and sunk my spoon deep into the chunky concoction.

Very tasty.

What did you leave out, I asked Pauline.

"Salt," she said. That struck me as odd: How could someone who's the salt of the earth forget that ingredient?

While the ladies at the doll show were a treat to be around, that couldn't be said for the dolls. The scene of hundreds of dolls staring at you with their beady little eyes is like walking into a poorly written Stephen King novel. I know some of these dolls are collectibles, but they still made my skin crawl.

One of the priciest was a 1916 German doll. It stood some three or four feet tall and had stringy, sooty black hair that hung down over a sickly pale-gray face. Only a mother, or in this case an owner, could love that creation. With a price tag of $650, that's a doll whose shadow will never darken my doorway.

A few Barbies, though, exchanged hands. I even think the "Barbie for President" might have sold, but the Barbie dressed in silver sequins — think Michael Jackson — did not.

I only found one Ken doll, called "Malibu Ken," and he was definitely scary — bare-chested with a roasty chestnut tan and funky-looking shorts. I couldn't quite get up the courage to buy him, but I did fork over $5 for a G.I. Joe doll with frizzed-out hair. Since the money went to the Salvation Army, I decided to deck him out with a pair of plastic shoes I purchased from a Baby Toothie hoarder.

Let's face it. I don't have what it takes to be a doll collector. But I just might have the chutzpah to be a seller after taking in $100 that day.

One of my more unusual sales happened when a lady stopped by my table and became fascinated with several small dolls from India, dressed as if they had just stepped out of a Rudyard Kipling storybook.

"There's no price on these," she said. "How much are they?"

I said five or 10 dollars, whatever you want to give. It all goes to a scholarship fund, I added.

She opened her purse and out spilled a $20 bill.

"How much again," she asked.

I didn't hesitate.

"Ten each," I said firmly, and grabbed the 20 out of her hand.

Out of one eye, I swear I saw the redhead smile.

# Senior prank rekindles memories of past exploits

*June 2, 1996*

P arents call them the Unlucky Thirteen.
That number represents the 13 Eisenhower High School students who were nabbed by police as they carried out an annual ritual — the senior prank. Although the incident took place nearly a month ago, it's still the talk of the town. Ike parents have lined up along two opposing battle lines, one side urging leniency and the other calling for the guillotine.

It all started in routine fashion when a reporter told me about a break-in at Eisenhower. It was listed in the daily Yakima police report. Police had taken 13 students into custody after the seniors had illegally entered the school using, of all things, a set of keys. Apparently some of the pranksters were children of Ike teachers.

Before the police had arrived, the Unlucky Thirteen had set out on their night of mischief, raiding lockers, removing books and tossing them around the cafeteria in what I see was an obvious attempt to thwart the librarian's Dewey Decimal System. Bottles of bleach were later found in a car, supposedly to be used to burn into a soccer field the number "96" as a final testament to their senior prank.

Ten days after the break-in, Yakima County Prosecutor Jeff Sullivan entered the fracas. In what has to be classified as one of the more oddball news conferences, Sullivan told a roomful of reporters that he would be filing charges against 10 of the teens, all 18 years old. He would recommend to the judge, though, that if they stay out of trouble during the next six months, shell out about $80 in restitution and do 20 hours of community service, the criminal charges would be wiped off their records forever.

What's going on here? When I first heard about the Ike senior prank, I shrugged my shoulders. No big deal. But after my 83rd phone call from a disgruntled Ike parent — either mad at school administrators for being too soft or angered at us in the news media for blowing the story out of proportion — I realized I was wrong.

Senior pranks are big business. It's a rite of graduation. Apparently you can't get a diploma without taking part in one.

Where I went to high school in the suburbs north of Chicago, senior pranks never reached the hall-of-fame status that they do here. But that changed in 1965 during the fall of my senior year after a bitterly fought football game between my school, Glenbrook North, and our most hated foe and cross-town rival, Glenbrook South. Our varsity squad got hammered during the game. The injured football players, including myself, littered the sidelines like a scene out of the movie, "Gone With the Wind."

After the game, a group of my friends — there were five of us, so naturally we called ourselves "The Fifths" — got together to discuss how to seek revenge. Jim Roach, one of our more enigmatic and taciturn members of "The Fifths," broke the wall of silence created by our gloom.

"Let's show those guys at South we mean business," he growled menacingly, holding up a clenched fist for all of us to see.

Emboldened by his call to arms, we cried out in unison: "The tower!"

The tower meant the industrial water tower located across the highway from Glenbrook South. It held a mythical charm, something akin to Mount Everest for climbers. For years we had talked about scaling the 170-foot water tower and painting some catchy phrase around its majestic circumference. We knew that that time had come.

On our way to the water tower, Mike Yunker, my best friend, made a brief side trip to his house where he retrieved a can of paint from his dad's treasure trove of paint paraphernalia. Mike's dad, an insufferable expert on home improvements, had hundreds of gallons of paint in every hue imaginable. Mike grabbed something with a catchy name — "radiant bone white enamel."

After scaling a perimeter fence topped with barbed wire, we reached the base of the behemoth water tower. A narrow, rusty ladder hung from its side, leading to a metal grating high above. Mike gamely scaled the rungs, the gallon of radiant bone white enamel dangling from one hand. It was a heroic sight.

"We made it," Mike called down minutes later as he reached that heavenly perch. Droplets of enamel paint filtered down as Mike and Brian David, a bantamweight varsity wrestler, worked their magic with two big paintbrushes. Five minutes later they were done. To mark the event, Mike twirled the can of paint high over his head and tossed it into the crisp autumn air. It thudded to the ground, lost in a field of scrub grass and broken bottles.

As we hurried back to the car, we lingered a moment to see what Mike and Brian had created. It wasn't Shakespeare, but in a bizarre way oddly eloquent. There in the thin silvery glow of night, against the pale blue backdrop of the water tank's metal facing, were two words: "South Sucks."

When we attended high school the following Monday, our escapade was the only thing students, and teachers, were talking about.

Later that afternoon, though, our celebrity status unraveled. Police officers arrived at school and escorted my best friend, Mike, into the principal's office. Our moment of glory had quickly turned into prolonged agony. It turns out the "radiant white bone enamel" proved to be our undoing. In searching the field around the tower for evidence, the police spied a gallon-sized can of paint. But this was no ordinary can of paint. It was a special blend that Mike's dad had professionally mixed. The can even had its own coded number, which the police traced back to its owner, then to his son, and finally to "The Fifths."

Punishment was swift. We had to pay $575 to get our two-word slogan painted over. Thankfully the company, which owned the water tower, didn't want to press charges. Our parents grounded us for what I regarded as "life plus eternity." Still, throughout the corridors of our alma mater, we were always greeted with admiration from our fellow classmates.

Although much has changed in the intervening 30 years between our tower painting and the Eisenhower senior prank, there is one unassailable truth that still holds firm. If you get caught, you pay the price. When the Eisenhower seniors unlocked the doors to their school, they crossed a point of no return. Criminal trespassing means criminal trespassing, regardless of how well connected your parents may be or whether you are a star athlete or class leader.

Yes, much has been said about the Ike senior prank, and little of it has been enlightening. The most vicious, ill-tempered claptrap has come from Ike parents eager to blame just about everyone except the students caught in the prank.

One of their favorite targets is Davis High School, Ike's cross-town rival (thank goodness there are no water towers in the area.) These belligerent parents have wondered why we in the news media haven't done anything about a senior prank that took place several weeks ago at Davis. Apparently five seniors were caught on a Sunday morning hurling garbage and ketchup around the high school's open-air courtyard. School administrators did what they could. They suspended the students from school for several days.

The police, though, had nothing to go on. They didn't even list the incident in their daily crime report. That's because no crime was committed. The students did not break into any public building nor did they trespass. Remember, it's an open courtyard. Also, the city has no ordinance making the act of littering a crime. So no charges were possible.

Nonetheless, the rumors persist; the phone calls and complaints continue.

"I wish people would get this involved when we get low test scores," bemoaned an exasperated Karen Garrison, Davis principal.

Seniors at Eisenhower and Davis high schools will graduate later this week and move ahead with their lives. So, too, should their parents.

# Lighting up the sky at 33,000 feet

*This is the way the world ends*
*Not with a bang but a whimper.*
— FROM "THE HOLLOW MEN" BY T.S. ELIOT

*November 4, 2012*

I t's never a good sign when you're standing in line to board an airplane and a fellow passenger is on her cell phone telling her husband: "And in case our plane crashes, the flight number is 856."

My wife, Leslie, poked fun at her and I brushed it off as a quirky comment coming at the end of a wonderful two-week trip to Kauai, where the tropics greeted us with sunshine and bartenders served up a colorful array of Mai Tais adorned with fresh slices of pineapple.

And for the first five hours and 15 minutes, everything was going well on our return flight to Seattle. Then came the pilot's mumbled warning over the intercom telling us to expect some turbulence during our descent.

Why does the mere mention of the word "turbulence" cause a plane to pitch wildly about? That's what happened to Flight 856 as we suddenly dropped down into a bank of clouds, which obliterated the view out our starboard porthole. Another series of jolts had our Boeing 737 jetliner bouncing like a pickup down a rutted mountain road.

Then came a flash of light.

"What was that," Leslie asked.

The next word I uttered is something you never, ever want to say while plunging toward earth from 33,000 feet.

"Lightning," I said, my voice barely audible above the sound of wind buffeting the jet.

Though it was hard to imagine, a bolt of lightning had indeed struck outside our window. It flashed hot and white and was gone in the blink of an eye, leaving no trace except for a palpable fear spreading among the passengers. I vaguely remembered reading a story about how modern jetliners are designed to withstand a direct lightning strike. Then again I also remember that a plane did crash in the late 1960s and investigators pinned the blame on a single culprit — a thunderbolt.

Remarkably our plane didn't drop like a stone nor did the interior lights flicker. We simply continued our steep descent, the fierceness of the storm we had entered continuing to pitch us violently from side to side.

I gazed out the window and strained to see the city lights of Seattle below. If they appear, we are saved, I thought to myself. Yes, I was deep into what psychologists would call "panic mode." I knew I had to divert my attention from the fact a moment ago lightning had blasted the side of our jet, leaving us mired in an impenetrable cloud with nowhere to go but down.

So I did what comes natural to me — I blabbered on incessantly, making small talk with Leslie.

And we had much to talk about following our first trip to the garden isle of Kauai. We could have chatted about the many hours we spent snorkeling along the beaches of Poipu where we came upon colorful creatures like the Reef Triggerfish with its pinkish snout and the yellow-banded Moorish Idol.

Yes, we could have reminisced about the treats we had feasted on, from Bubba burgers to Hawaiian shaved ice and my personal favorite — sashimi-grade ahi (raw tuna).

Or we could have commiserated over our arduous hike at Waimea Canyon where we stumbled through thickets of wild ginger. We expected a few rain showers that day and we weren't disappointed since the canyon lies in the shadow of Mount Wai'ale'ale whose summit has the distinction of being the wettest spot in the world with an average annual rainfall of 432 inches.

And we easily could have entertained our fellow passengers with a description of our trip to the quirky town of Hanalei on the island's northern coastline. It's home to Tahiti Nui, a nondescript bar and restaurant that's as famous as the Roslyn Café once was during the heydays of the TV hit, "Northern Exposure." Leslie and I each ordered a Mai Tai, the same fruity rum drink that George

Clooney was treated to during a scene from the Academy-Award nominated movie, "The Descendants." We sat at an outdoor table and peered through an open window at the U-shaped bar where Clooney had sat shoulder-to-shoulder with actor Beau Bridges during a pivotal scene in the movie.

Yes, that would have been a fun conversation to share with others as the plane jostled wildly about.

Instead, we talked about assault weapons.

It all had to do with a sold-out Madonna concert at Key Arena we attended two days before our trip to Kauai. I bought the tickets as a birthday gift for Leslie.

It didn't start well. In fact, I had my doubts we would ever see the aging rock star. Finally, at 10:30 p.m. — about the time I usually head off for bed — Madonna took the stage armed with an assault rifle and a pistol. She then proceeded to gun down an endless stream of black-clad assailants in tempo with her song, "Gang Bang." Each time she pulled the trigger, blood splattered across a mammoth video screen behind her.

"Was that really necessary," lamented a concertgoer sitting next to us.

That same thought came to mind when I gazed heavenward during our roller-coaster ride aboard Flight 856: Was that lightning bolt really necessary?

Then it happened. The clouds suddenly parted to reveal a nest of diamonds below, the twinkling lights of Seattle.

When the plane's wheels touched down on the tarmac, a flight attendant asked for a show of appreciation for how the pilots handled our far-from-routine descent. Applause and huzzahs quickly echoed throughout the cabin.

Now that's the way to end a trip to paradise — not with a thunderclap but a handclap.

# Pilgrimage to Memphis leaves you all shook up

*March 26, 2006*

A thin, wiry haberdasher who likes designer ties, 78-year-old Bernard Lansky could have retired years ago. But why? Business is great at his store, nestled within the famed Peabody Hotel in downtown Memphis, Tennessee. Anyway, selling top-of-the line clothes is only part of his trade. What he's really known for is dressing the King of Rock 'n' Roll.

On a trip last month to Memphis I came face to face with the one and only "Mister Lansky." That's how Elvis Presley would address him when they met. And that would be often.

Lansky once designed a special outfit for Elvis to wear at his high school prom — a pink coat, black pants and a pink-and-black cummerbund. He even came to Elvis' rescue when the young crooner made his historic appearance in 1956 on the "Ed Sullivan Show," which was seen by a record 60 million viewers. Lansky put Elvis in a fancy suit even though he couldn't pay for it. That didn't bother Lansky. He knew the kid was going places.

Within a year, Elvis would become a millionaire. Twenty-one years later, Lansky would be there at Elvis' side again, but for a much sadder occasion — attending the pop star's funeral.

"He was a heck of a nice guy," Lansky told a Forbes magazine reporter recently. "I put him in his first suit, and I put him in his last suit."

So there I was standing in front of Mister Lansky. How could I resist when he said, "Can I help you?" Destiny was calling. I just had to buy something.

Lansky showed me a rack of silk ties. Their $100 price tags scared me off. Then I glanced at the Tommy Bahama shirts, their Hawaiian patterns sleek on silk. But at $140 a pop, I decided to search for an item more suitable for someone in a lower-income bracket.

"Forty percent off what a deal," I muttered to myself as I read the sign above a rack of brightly colored dress shirts. I picked out the gaudiest of the lot and headed to the cash register. I didn't dare take a look at the price. I knew Elvis never would have.

"That'll be $122," the clerk said coolly.

My heart pounded as I opened my wallet and fumbled for a credit card. Good grief, I muttered to myself, this is the most expensive shirt I've ever bought in my life.

I had no choice. I signed my name — it was in red ink — and darted out the door. That's the power of Elvis. You do things you never thought you would.

Next stop — a trip to Graceland.

Getting to the mansion is no easy feat. It's some 10 miles from downtown Memphis. Shuttles from our hotel cost upwards of $40. I decided to take the less expensive route — public transit. At $1.40 (or $120.60 less than the shirt I had bought the day before), it was my best buy in Memphis.

Just before the bus turned down Elvis Presley Boulevard, we skirted by Sun Studio, a small triangular-shaped building that marked the birthplace of Elvis' recording career. It was there that a teenage Elvis recorded a song for his mother. Hearing the young singer was producer Sam Phillips, who signed him to a recording contract. A year later, Phillips would sell that contract to RCA Victor, and Elvis would then purchase, for a tidy $100,000, a sprawling 14-acre home — Graceland Mansion — that today welcomes more than 600,000 visitors a year.

After the bus dropped me off across from Graceland, I made a beeline, not for the ticket office to book a tour, but for a small restaurant next to a row of Elvis souvenir shops. I walked right up to the lady taking orders and picked the top item on the menu. It was pure Elvis.

"I'll take the fried peanut butter and banana sandwich," I called out. His cook, Mary Jenkins, would fry up the concoction for Elvis at all hours of the day and night. (Here are the ingredients Mary would whip together: two large bananas, peeled and mashed; one cup peanut butter; six slices of white bread; one stick of butter).

Though there was still a chill in the air, I sat outside and took a big bite out of the sandwich. Mildly unpleasant, I thought to myself. A large glass of sweetened iced tea helped me to finish it off. A craving suddenly gripped me: Bring on the jelly doughnuts.

Later, I booked a tour of the 1970s-era mansion, but worried it would be tacky and tasteless. I shouldn't have. There's a reason why Graceland is one of the most visited homes in America, next only to the White House.

The tour was sheer joy. Leslie and I spent nearly two hours walking through the two-story mansion, ending up at the gravesite for Elvis and the rest of his family. With headsets on for the audio tour, we entered the home and stepped toward the living room, with the baby grand piano in the background, white carpeting throughout, and, on a nearby table, a picture of Elvis' parents, Gladys and Vernon.

Everything is as it was back on Aug. 16, 1977, when Elvis died. Very eerie. But for those legions of Elvis fans throughout the world, it's anything but weird. This is sacred ground, like a holy shrine where the devoted come to pray at the garish altar of the 20th century's most famous pop star.

Standing at the bottom of the stairs, I looked up to see a stunning portrait of a young Elvis, his white tuxedo shirt opened at the collar. What a handsome young man he was, a gifted singer not only of rock, but also of blues, country and his most favorite, gospel. No one is allowed up these stairs that lead into the private quarters where the 42-year-old Elvis died.

Bernard Lansky was allowed upstairs. He was one of the few who was given that privilege when Elvis was alive. He would drop off clothes for the King to try on. But what connection did I have with Elvis? It seems like everyone has one. I love his music like "Burnin' Love" and "It's Now or Never." But where did his life intersect with mine?

I found that in the oddest of places — the famed Jungle Room, where Elvis would rehearse his songs because of its great acoustics. The room's Polynesian furniture definitely had that '70s look. Leaning on the arm of a fur-lined, black-and-white striped chair rested a guitar and, next to it, a stuffed Panda bear. On the floor, and yes on the ceiling as well, was the signature household fixture of the era — algae-green shag carpet.

What a happy coincidence. That's the same carpet I have in my home in Yakima.

# Impersonators are queens (and Kings) of The Strip

*April 8, 2012*

I t didn't matter if you had bought a $250 ticket in advance to attend a Celine Dion concert at Caesar's Palace. She was a no-show. Struck down by worn-out vocal cords, the celebrated singer had to cancel her Las Vegas concerts until June.

That didn't stop us on our recent vacation. We headed across Las Vegas Boulevard and saw Celine in person. She waved to us and then belted out her signature song, "My Heart Will Go On," from the blockbuster movie "Titanic." Not bad for $45 front-row tickets. But there was more. How about this lineup: Cher, Diana Ross, Bette Midler and Madonna. A curvaceous Dolly Parton also strutted her stuff after being introduced by a saucy-tongued Joan Rivers, resplendent in her skintight sequin dress.

A concert for the ages? Not really. Credit Frank Marino's "Divas Las Vegas" for the cavalcade of stars. Marino has lit up stages in Sin City for the past 27 years, making him the longest-running Vegas headliner of all time. And with his stable of a dozen or so female impersonators, there's never a dull moment. We even witnessed a reincarnation of the late Whitney Houston. As we found out, when impersonating celebrities, anything is possible.

"If the idea of a bunch of guys traipsing around in fishnet stockings and feather boas gives you the willies, opt for something more conventional," reads an excerpt from "Las Vegas 2012: The Unofficial Guide."

My wife, Leslie, couldn't care less about conventional and persuaded me to see the Divas over "Phantom of the Opera." When we arrived for the 10 p.m. show at the Imperial Palace, an aged casino set back from the busy Vegas Boulevard, we took an escalator up to a second-floor showroom and were greeted by a larger-than-life Tina Turner. With her hair teased out to the size of a huge beach ball, the 6-foot-plus Tina gave me a hug. While in her embrace, I could make out in the distance the not-so-dulcet sounds of someone belting out a Neil Diamond tune. Egad, it was a karaoke bar.

What amazed me about the show, besides the impeccable makeup and wardrobes worn by the impersonators, was the audience. They seemed so normal. A married couple in their late 50s sat across from us. They had driven down from British Columbia. The husband was a farmer. I asked him if he felt a bit uneasy in the company of guys gussied up as women. He shook his head.

"This is my third time seeing the show," he exclaimed with a devilish grin. His favorite? Cher.

Soon we were all laughing at Marino's impression of the acerbic Joan Rivers. He reminded me of a vaudeville comedian who, whenever he exhaled, spewed out an endless stream of one-liners.

"They even named a street after me in Vegas," Marino said. "You might drive down it while you're here. It also goes both ways." A groan issued up from the audience except for the farmer from British Columbia. He had tears welling up in his eyes from laughing so hard.

Why do so many unassuming adults find these female impersonators so entertaining? It's as if the Real McCoys are somehow disappointing, that they are not real enough. How weird is that? Marino even sells a Divas cookbook. Naturally, I bought one.

A trip to Las Vegas, though, would never be complete without seeing an Elvis impersonator and there is none bigger than Big Elvis, who once tipped the scales at 960 pounds. He has slimmed down to 450 pounds thanks to dieting, walks in the park and swimming laps in his backyard pool. OK, he's still more than a fifth of a ton but the guy, Pete Vallee, can really belt out the Elvis hits. His vibrant baritone voice has vaulted him into Time magazine's Top 10 list of Elvis impersonators.

Big Elvis performs three times a day during the week for free at Bill's Gamblin' Hall and Saloon. The afternoon we saw him, the place was packed. Big Elvis was celebrating his 10th anniversary performing on the Strip.

After being treated to a rambling speech by his agent, Big Elvis asked his wife, Amanda, to dance for his next song. Part Hawaiian and part Filipino, the slim Amanda, who has ELVIS PRESLEY tattooed on her neck, swayed in rhythm to "Blue Hawaii." With many in the audience saluting the performance with raised bar glasses and beer bottles, Big Elvis turned to his wife and smiled. The room erupted in applause.

Yakima Valley residents are not immune to harboring warm feelings for impersonators. Danny Vernon, from the Seattle area, has brought his hip-swiveling Elvis to The Seasons Performance Hall in Yakima. Vernon offers a far more athletic version of Elvis the Pelvis than the sedentary Big Elvis, whose generous girth keeps him firmly planted in his gold-embroidered, high-back chair.

We've also had our share of female impersonators pay a visit to the Yakima Valley. Remember Dixie Longate and her "Tupperware Party" two years ago at The Seasons? It's hard to forget the sight of her showing us how to chug down alcohol-laced Jell-O shots, something she recommended for the next church social. Actor Kris Andersson created Dixie as a Tupperware sales gimmick in 2004 and suddenly found himself on the road, playing in front of sellout venues while still peddling a full line of kitchenware.

Yakima loved Dixie, so why not the Divas from Las Vegas? I figured if a Tupperware cross-dresser could fill the 400-seat Seasons, surely Joan Rivers could pack the 1,500-seat Capitol Theatre. So I hit a button marked "book the Diva" on Marino's website and sent a message.

"How about bringing Celine, Tina and the rest of your lady friends to Yakima," I wrote. "You would be a hit here."

Marino has yet to reply. I'm sure he's busy. I mean really, you don't get to be a top headliner on the Vegas Strip by sitting on your behind. Unless you're Big Elvis.

# A park-like setting

*September 16, 2012*

No wonder I rarely see anyone outside tending to his or her yard. It's hostile territory. We homeowners, who yearn for the splendors of green grass and prolific vegetable gardens, are battle-weary by the time September rolls along. Our bank accounts are depleted and our once verdant lawns are pockmarked with dead grass.

Let's face the truth: evil lurks between the blades of our Kentucky blue. Creating a park-like setting around your domicile is no easy task — dare I say, no walk in the park. Show any lack of resolve and the aphids and earwigs will eat you alive. Literally.

The list of potential pests and diseases attacking a lawn reads like the credits from a low-budget horror movie: necrotic ring spot, fusarium blight, sclerotinia dollar spot, strip smut and pythium blight.

Did I forget to mention a herd of cattle?

When we moved three years ago into our new home in Yakima's West Valley area, we knew we had our work cut out. The lawn looked like the face of the moon — with large craters dug into the turf. My first thought was an invasion of moles.

It turns out the perpetrators were a bit larger — by about a thousand pounds. Our neighbor described a bizarre scene when he woke up and saw a herd of cattle grazing in his backyard. The herd then moved over to our yard and set up camp. They dug up the ground with their sharp hooves and munched on what had been green tufts of grass until our former homeowner ran them off the property. But the damage had been done.

So I tried to patch the turf with new seed. It seemed to work until the following summer when I noticed more dead spots in the lawn, even after a steady round of fertilizer.

"Hey, what happened to our park-like setting," my wife, Leslie, inquired at the time.

Fearing I might be spending the night in our garden shed, I made a desperate call to a lawn care professional. He took one look at the dead spots in the lawn and announced his verdict: billbugs.

Yes, you're right to ask, "What's a billbug?" My reply: very expensive. They are ugly, too. Here's how one landscape specialist on the Internet described these pests: "These nasty little larvae have a ferocious appetite for turf. ... Billbug damage is identified by the white 'frass' (a white excrement that resembles Christmas tree flocking) found in the thatch layer." It lacks poetry but the message is clear. Don't dawdle. Kill the pests.

Two hundred dollars later and our lawn began to show remarkable improvement. A park-like setting seemed attainable.

Then came the spring of 2012. Wet and cold lingered into June and suddenly our lawn began to deteriorate once again. More billbugs? No way. This time there was fungus among us.

Again we received a home visit by a lawn care doctor who grimly probed our turf and prescribed a costly remedy: $700 to spread a quarter-inch thick carpet of organic compost over our entire lawn. Or we could do it ourselves.

I chose the cheaper option. Little did I know it would require hauling in 23 heavy bags of compost and spending an entire week, from dawn to dusk, raking the material into the lawn. The compost is supposed to nurture friendly microorganisms, which then feast on the fungi. Sounds cannibalistic, but that's lawn care. It's no trip to Disneyland.

Just when victory seemed in sight, another calamity arose. I noticed a small section of grass in the backyard appeared to have been dug up.

I searched for clues in my nearby raised bed garden. That's where I found several green bean stalks sheared off at ground level. Next to the green beans there was a small hole dug deep into the soil. Yes, we had been invaded by one of the most dreaded rodents known to gardeners — the ground squirrel.

While you may have visions of cute, furry animals skittering about the yard, think again. They are a menace to society, ranking right up there with the famed gopher from the 1980 cult movie, "Caddyshack." No wonder Bill Murray's character, Carl Spackler, finally resorted to plastic explosives, turning a lush golf course into a scene from World War I.

There's not much you can do about ground squirrels. Though stores sell traps, it's against the law to cage squirrels and cart them off to a new zip code. You either live with them or, as one hardware store employee recommended, you can poison them. Both are bad options.

So I decided to take a more organic approach. After reading lengthy testimonials on several blog sites about its beneficial attributes, I purchased a spray bottle containing — I'm not making this up — coyote urine. We're talking pure uric acid here. The stuff is sold right next to the hardware store's animal traps you're not allowed to use.

Guess what? Coyote urine works. I rank it right up there with duct tape as something every homeowner can't live without.

Though I no longer had to worry about ground squirrels gnawing at my green beans, that didn't mean our backyard was rid of the furry freeloader. About a week after I applied the miracle urine to the perimeter of our garden, Leslie spotted our resident ground squirrel standing on its hind legs atop our deck. Such audacity.

Later that night a most unusual thing happened. At about 1 a.m. we heard several loud explosions outside our bedroom window. The night sky lit up. Leslie dove for cover, fearing someone was outside with a gun. I had another idea. Maybe our ground squirrel got electrocuted by a nearby power line?

Though neighbors down the street believe a couple of teens had tossed M-80 fireworks near our home, I still think the squirrel got fried. Want proof? We haven't seen the animal since then.

In this ceaseless battle pitting mere mortals against billbugs and fairy rings, it never hurts to have a Pacific Power line in the vicinity. It trumps coyote urine every time.

# Even novices can learn to appreciate art of fly fishing

*"If our father had had his way, nobody who did not know how to fish would be allowed to disgrace a fish by catching him."*
*-- Norman Maclean, "A River Runs Through It"*

*May 6, 2012*

Fly fishing takes patience, finesse, great eyesight, dexterity, smarts — all of which I lack.

Maybe that explains why after taking a fly fishing lesson, I walked away wondering if the instructor had said "caddis" or "caboose." That probably explains why I have never found an artificial fly with a caboose. They don't exist. It does, though, explain why my attempts at fly fishing are more like a train wreck than a ballet of coordinated moves. I'm a klutz, and in my hands, a fly rod becomes a deadly weapon.

I grew up in the Midwest and was taught that the art of fishing meant spearing a hapless earthworm with a barbed hook and waiting for something with dorsal fins to take a bite. The notion of using artificial flies seemed so — well, let's just state the obvious -- sissy. Really what's the point of it all? A lure made out of elk hair and peacock feathers? What about pink-dyed marshmallows? They've never failed me.

It turns out history is on the side of those who fly fish. The first recorded use of an artificial fly occurred in the second century along the banks of the Astraeus River in Macedonia, north of Greece. Writing on papyrus, the Roman Claudius Aelianus provided a play-by-play account of the historic meeting between a rainbow trout and an artificial fly:

"They fasten red wool ... round a hook, and fit on to the wool two feathers which grow under a cock's wattles, and which in color are like wax. Their rod is 6 feet long, and their line is the same length. Then they throw their snare, and the fish, attracted and maddened by the color, comes straight at it, thinking from the pretty sight to gain a dainty mouthful; when, however, it opens its jaws, it is caught by the hook, and enjoys a bitter repast, a captive."

This poetic tribute comes from William Radcliff's 1921 tome, "Fishing from the Earliest Times." How quaint, but trust me it's nothing like a scene from the hit movie, "A River Runs Through It," when a young Brad Pitt casts an artificial fly for what seemed like a quarter-of-a-mile across Montana's Big Blackfoot River and hooks a broad-shouldered rainbow, which then performs a series of somersaults.

Like so many other armchair anglers, I became fascinated with the sport after seeing the movie. Based on a novella by Norman Maclean, "A River Runs Through It" is about two brothers (Pitt portrays the wild and self-destructive younger brother) being raised in the wilds of Montana by their father, a Presbyterian minister who treats rainbow trout as saintly creatures.

"In our family, there was no clear line between religion and fishing," says the older brother.

My initial foray into fly fishing ended up with more curses than hallelujahs. It took place several years ago on a fall afternoon when I ventured, hip waders and a new fly rod in hand, to the Yakima River. I lifted up the fly rod and performed what I thought was a perfect imitation of Brad Pitt's back cast.

The artificial fly zipped over my head, never to be seen again. It ended up high in a willow tree. I jerked down hard and felt the thin leader line snap. After muttering a few expletives gleaned from my two years in the Army, I reached into my backpack for another fly and realized I had left my box of flies at home.

So ended my first day of fly fishing.

Still, the allure of tricking a trout into swallowing a fake fly proved irresistible. This time, my wife, Leslie, suggested I take lessons. She figured while it might not improve my chances at catching a fish, it would greatly reduce the possibility of bodily harm to myself.

So I signed up last summer for a lesson through Red's Fly Shop, which is next to the Canyon River Ranch midway between Ellensburg and Yakima. On a grassy knoll between the lodge and the river, I learned how to cast a fly without wrapping it around the limb of a tree.

It's simple really. You tie onto your fly line a strike indicator called a Thingamabobber followed by two artificial flies — a stonefly nymph (it's wide-bodied with thin, dangling arms and legs) and a minuscule fly no bigger than a kernel of corn. It's called the Prince of Darkness. How's that for marketing? I bought five of them.

A few weeks later, I was back on the banks of the Yakima River, testing what I had learned in class. I let out some fly line and whipped the fly rod in front of me from left to right, sending the Thingamabobber with its trailing flies upstream. The orange bobber floated past me. It was magical.

Then the bobber slipped under a swirl of water and disappeared. What's going on? I figured I had snagged a rock. I lifted the rod. Suddenly the fly line ripped through my fingers. "Holy mackerel," I yelled. I had hooked a rainbow, and it was a monster.

Instead of heading farther downstream, though, the trout swam directly at me. With the fly rod held high over my head, I tried to gather in the fly line but failed miserably. It got twisted around my neck and shoulders. How could this happen? Panic set in. I noticed the fly line had gone slack. This is not good.

I gave the line a tug. What's this? The trout was still hooked. The leviathan must have realized this, too, for its next move was to head like a jet ski downstream. After ripping off 50 or so feet of fly line, the fish rose into the air, its silver flanks flashing in the sun. For the next five minutes, I fought this brute in the strong current of the Yakima River. Three times I brought it near my feet, and three times it headed back into the rapids. Finally, it corkscrewed high into the autumn air, some 20 yards from me, and broke off my Prince of Darkness.

I stood there trembling, exhausted but excited as well. So that's fly fishing? Not bad. I ran my fingers through my hair and struck a pose that Brad Pitt had taken after he also lost a big trout. Cold water spilled over my boots. It felt good to be alive.

# Don't let wildlife encounter end up as a YouTube video

*November 14, 2010*

I wonder what a bighorn sheep is thinking when it sees a clumsy 62-year-old man climb up a rocky slope, his backpack slipping to one side and his hiking boots dislodging a shower of rocks beneath him.

Pity perhaps. Or a longing to be left alone.

But I wasn't about to abandon my vantage point. Not yet. I had seen the pair of bighorns clinging to a cliff several hundred yards away. I trained my binoculars on the ram, his curled horns motionless as he stared back at me. He seemed to be suspended in air.

I waved my hand. Maybe a friendly gesture will warm them up, I thought.

No reaction. They viewed me as they would any intruder, especially someone who dared to wear a Chicago Cubs baseball cap, with utter disdain.

Coming upon the two bighorns was an unexpected treat for me while hiking a few weeks ago up the western slopes of Cleman Mountain near Naches. In the fall, I like to venture out to the 5,000-foot-peak, where autumn leaves along the creek beds are bright and the air is brisk. About two miles into the hike a stand of aspen trees rises up and crowds the path worn by hiking boots and animal hooves. It's a sublime, cathedral-like oasis before taking the final ascent.

I'm not a well-traveled explorer but I realize close encounters with wildlife can become dangerous, turning an afternoon jaunt into a video on YouTube. Right now one of the most popular on the website is a clip of an enraged deer pummeling a hunter with its hooves. Very graphic.

These run-ins can also lead to tragedy, as it did when a 300-pound mountain goat gored a hiker to death last month along a trail near Port Angeles.

Though my run-ins with wild animals have never been captured on video or made national headlines, my scariest encounter certainly had the potential. It happened in the late spring of 1973 after I was discharged from the Army at Fort Sam Houston in San Antonio. The day I received my official papers, my friend and I headed west in hopes of getting out of Texas as fast as possible. Of course, that's not easily done when driving a four-cylinder Volkswagen Beetle overloaded with clothes, books, tent and assorted camping gear.

We reached the western edge of the state where it borders with New Mexico. On the horizon rose a magnificent limestone peak — El Capitan. While Yosemite may have its own famous mountain with the same name, the Texas equivalent is just as majestic and inspiring.

"Let's climb it," I said as we pulled into one of the campsites at Guadalupe Mountains National Park.

The next morning a park ranger stopped by and handed us a flier. It read: "Beware of cougars." He described several recent sightings of the unpredictable beast.

"Do they attack humans?" I asked.

"Sometimes," he responded.

Not encouraging news, but my friend and I quickly calculated the odds of us, who both grew up in the suburbs of Chicago, meeting face-to-face with a cougar. It came out to zero. So off we went.

We reached a small stand of trees and decided to take a lunch break. My friend got a bit too relaxed while leaning against a tree and fell fast asleep. So I headed out on a short side trip across a nearby ridge. When I reached a nice viewing point, I sat down and rested against a large rock.

That didn't last long. I heard a noise behind me. It's the kind of sound you never want to hear in the wilderness — that of a carnivore growling a few feet away. The heavy exhale came again. It was clearly an animal. A very big animal. In my mind's eye I imagined the creature's gaping maw with large incisors dripping with thick saliva, or blood.

It's a cougar!

I froze. What do I do now? Then came another exhale from the unseen beast.

Sheer panic set in. I reached for a Swiss Army knife lodged deep in my pants' pocket. But what good would that do? I could hear my first sergeant yelling in my ear: "Good luck scaring off a cougar with that butter knife."

So I held my ground. It was a Texas standoff, me against the cougar.

A minute passed by. No heavy breathing. Another minute. Again, the only sound was my heart beating at 190 thumps a minute.

I waited for what seemed an eternity — actually it was only 10 minutes — and figured something had to be done. I couldn't sit here all day. I gingerly inched my body around a corner of the boulder and took a peek. Nothing. No cougar. Suddenly a message telegraphed itself across my distraught brain: "Get out of here, you idiot!"

The next morning we headed north to Carlsbad Caverns, where we were greeted with the sight of what seemed like a million bats flying overhead. One zipped by my ear. I was beginning to think that staying in the Army would have been much safer.

So when it comes to animals in the wild, I prefer them stuck on a ledge like the bighorns I saw near Cleman Mountain. I certainly don't want them any closer. The only breathing I want to hear is the sigh I make when I reach my car and fumble for the keys.

# Trying to get a good book review like being lost in Amazon

*January 13, 2013*

After pouring a cup of freshly brewed coffee for my wife, Leslie, I asked her for a favor.

"Could you write a review of my book on Amazon," I pleaded. "It's been six weeks and nothing's been posted."

Before Thanksgiving, I received 250 copies of my first-ever book, "Counting Crows: Stories of Love, Laughter and Loss." The book garnered numerous flattering comments on Facebook and I had a book-signing event at Inklings Bookshop in Yakima that was a huge success.

Still, "Counting Crows" added up to zilch on Amazon, the world's largest online retailer. That meant no 5-star ratings and no catchy one-liners — "It's a page turner." All I had to show for two years of work compiling the book was a bleak note from Amazon telling everyone who ventured in search of "Counting Crows" that no one had reviewed it.

So to break into the win column, I turned to Leslie. I figured if anyone could give the 320-page tome an in-depth review, it would be my wife. Leslie has always been my toughest critic and proved invaluable in the final editing stages. She's never been timid when it comes to sharing her opinions and would challenge me whenever a phrase or word did not meet with her approval.

"This makes no sense," she declared one day after reading one of my newspaper columns contained in the book. "Get rid of it."

While patiently waiting for Leslie's reply, I glanced down at the front page of the Sunday New York Times. A headline caught my attention: "5 Stars for Mom's New Book? Amazon Purge Stirs an Uproar."

Good grief, what had I stepped into this time?

The news story detailed how Amazon was trying to clean up its act with respect to phony book reviews. Apparently its website is awash in them. The ruckus started after a group of authors banded together and signed a petition titled "No Sock Puppets Here Please." The puppet reference has to do with authors who have used deceitful methods to get book reviews posted online. Not surprisingly, these reviews all boasted 5-star ratings.

When several of these writers confessed their sins, outrage among their fellow scribes flooded the blogosphere. Amazon took note of the potential public relations nightmare and struck back, with a vengeance. No soft sock puppets here. The mega bookseller put on the boxing gloves and came out swinging. It began giving the heave-ho to thousands of book reviews. No longer would friends and family members be allowed to post reviews.

Worse yet, Amazon singled out the starving artists of the world — those authors, like myself, who self-publish through independent book publishers. According to a recent story on Forbes.com, a well-intentioned author tried to review a fellow writer's book. Amazon responded with this smack down: "We do not allow reviews on behalf of a person or company with a financial interest in the product or a directly competing product. This includes authors, artists, publishers, manufacturers, or third-party merchants selling the product. We have removed your reviews as they are in violation of our guidelines. We will not be able to go into further detail about our research."

It gets crazier. Take, for instance, the case of Todd Rutherford, who turned from failed publicist to rich publicist in 2010 when he decided to stop sending out requests for legitimate book reviews and instead wrote them himself. In doing so, he guaranteed 5-star reviews for all of his paid clients.

And Rutherford had many eager-to-be-reviewed authors clamoring for his services. In a story published last summer by The New York Times, this purveyor of pulp fiction sold 4,531 reviews and, at the height of his brief con game, was banking $28,000 a month.

Even after his house of canards fell apart, some of Rutherford's paid-for reviews were still posted on Amazon. Though Rutherford deleted reviews under his name, he hasn't told Amazon about the others he has penned under different aliases, arguing that he didn't consider those reviews as "necessarily fake." How's that for twisted logic?

It's sad to see what has befallen the once proud tradition of reviewing books and other creative forms of expression. I'm not ashamed to admit that my first stories to appear in a daily newspaper were movie reviews.

My humble start began in the summer of 1974 in Durango, Colorado, where I had found refuge after a two-year stint in the Army. I worked as a proofreader for the Durango Herald and decided to try my hand at writing. After spending long hours fretting over syntax and verb-subject agreement, I turned in reviews of the re-release of the Disney 1940 classic "Fantasia," an animated movie teeming with dancing hippos dressed as ballerinas, and Mel Brook's "Blazing Saddles," a farcical cowboy western, which featured a camp-fire scene where baked beans ruled and self-restraint didn't.

The editor nodded when I asked if he liked the reviews and soon they were published, much to my delight. So started my career in journalism.

However, I'm barely a blip on the radar screen when compared to reviewers like Harriet Klausner. The New York Times dubbed her "an Amazon Hall of Fame reviewer for the last 11 years and undoubtedly one of the most prolific reviewers in literary history."

Klausner, a 60-year-old retired librarian from Atlanta, recently posted her 28,366 book review, an incredible feat achieved by writing reviews at a rate of seven a day for more than a decade — without a break. The Times also calculated that 99.9 percent of her reviews fell between 4 or 5 stars. That's a lot of shout-outs.

So now back to Leslie. What would she do?

After I read her excerpts from the Times article about Amazon's supposedly new-and-improved review policy, she stared up at me and offered this succinct advice: "Get over yourself."

Little wonder writing is such a lonely profession. In a game of words with no clear victor, it appears you can't even count on your wife for a 5-star review.

# Cast of Characters

---

*"Maybe the best thing would be to forget being right
or wrong about people and just go along for the ride.
But if you can do that — well, lucky you."*
— PHILIP ROTH, AMERICAN NOVELIST

# Robertson family legacy still felt in Yakima Valley

*October 18, 1998*

It does seem odd in a museum filled with so much of the Yakima Valley, from antique apple bins to a neon "Yakima Cycle Shop" sign, that there would be artifacts from Africa, India, Egypt and beyond.

So the question didn't seem unusual at all when a woman asked me as I stood there gazing at a photograph of the Taj Mahal: "Who's Robertson? He seems to have traveled a lot."

How do you describe an icon?

I find it hard to believe that anyone who comes through the Yakima Valley is able to elude the Midas touch of the Robertson legend. It goes far beyond the Yakima Herald-Republic newspaper, which the Robertson family nurtured from its infancy. True, the passage of time has dimmed the Robertson name from the headlines. More than 26 years have gone by since the late Ted Robertson, heir to his father's newspaper empire here in Central Washington, last gazed upon a front page that he could call his own. Maybe that's why I snuck in a few minutes recently to revisit the newly refurbished Robertson exhibit at the Yakima Valley Museum. Like that woman wondering whom Robertson was, I wanted to be sure I didn't forget.

Creating a legacy by giving back to the community was a sweet obsession for the Robertsons. From the early years of this century, the Robertson name has been synonymous with the Yakima Valley, from the hallways of the Yakima Valley Museum to the Capitol Theatre, which never would have risen from the ashes of a disastrous fire had it not been for Ted's generosity.

A cursory scan of the expanded Robertson exhibit reveals a world far beyond the irrigated orchards of the Yakima Valley.

Along the south wall of the exhibit, a series of lists reveal what appears to be an index torn from the back pages of a world atlas. Ted and his second wife, Ruth, made globetrotting a full-time avocation. From 1961 to 1962, they visited Egypt, Greece, Turkey and Italy, then jumped to South America to take in Chile and Peru, where they stood together and gazed at the heavens from the steps of the famed Incan ruins of Machu Picchu.

Ted wrote extensively about his travels and sent back reams upon reams of correspondence to the Herald-Republic, which published them under the whimsical heading of "Touring with Ruth and Ted." Excerpts of these travelogues are interspersed within the treasure trove of souvenirs in the museum's exhibit.

For all the glitter that was Ted's trips to Rome and to countries rarely visited 30 years ago, it still doesn't match the one trip that brought his father here to Yakima. For without that long train trip on the Northern Pacific in 1898 by the elder Robertson, Ted's travels to Africa and the South Pacific never would have been possible.

And the same is true for the many riches that he later would bestow upon our Valley if his father, Wilbur Wade Robertson, had not decided to forego purchasing a small metro newspaper, The Seattle Times, and instead jumped aboard a train heading to North Yakima, a burgeoning agricultural community of 3,000 hardy souls.

When Robertson arrived in town in 1898, it was well past midnight. He could not find a room to rent so he did the next best thing. He settled for a short nap atop a billiard table at one of Yakima's finest saloons.

The next day was a Sunday, but it wasn't going to be a day of rest for the 31-year-old Robertson. He set out to buy The Republic, one of two weeklies in North Yakima (the city would later be renamed Yakima in 1918). The other newspaper, The Herald, was not for sale at the time. It would be another 12 years before Robertson would bring that newspaper under his ownership.

Robertson had to make a long, dusty seven-mile trek on foot in order to talk to one of The Republic partners. He wouldn't take no for an answer. He struck a deal to buy the weekly that afternoon, and the Robertson legacy had begun.

W.W. Robertson — "The Colonel"
Photo courtesy of Yakima Valley Museum

Although the museum exhibit devotes only one corner of the Robertson room to W.W. Robertson, it's clear from his steely-eyed gaze that he held a commanding presence in Ted's life.

As was the custom in those days when someone became publisher of a newspaper, the title "The Colonel" came along with the job. In the case of W.W. Robertson, the moniker suited him well. He ran the Robertson household with military precision, getting Ted and his older sister, Helen, up by 6 a.m. to do exercises, and always demanding breakfast and dinner at a set time. Leftovers were not allowed, and there was no idle chatter at the table, either. The Colonel never thought much of self-inflated egos.

"If you keep your mouth shut people won't know how dumb you really are," Ted recalls his father telling him.

The Colonel distinguished himself in other ways, too, especially while strolling down the streets of Yakima. In his memoir, "How the Twig Was Bent," Ted painted a colorful picture of his father's everyday appearance: "a bit over 6 feet tall, close to 200 pounds with broad shoulders, white hair, a white cap, cigar, loose sweater, baggy pants and bedroom slippers." It seems comfort meant more to the Colonel than being a businessman in a starchy white collar.

When it came to convictions, the Colonel held dearly to his Republican Party affiliations, writing editorials daily on the evils of rising taxes as he kept close reins on the newspaper's operations throughout the nearly four decades of his leadership. His devotion to work soon led him to construct sleeping quarters at the Herald-Republic, where he would dabble with culinary concoctions cooked atop a hot plate he had purchased for late-night meals. Only the roar and rumble of the presses early in the morning would stir the Colonel from his office-resting place.

Ted's introduction to the newspaper world started at the tender age of 9. His duties? For $2 a week, Ted got to sweep the floors and clean out the cuspidors where the pressmen had attempted, with varying degrees of success, to discharge the unsavory residue from their chewing tobacco.

"You are just another employee around here and are not entitled to any special privileges," the Colonel once told Ted.

After graduating from Harvard, Ted worked his way up the corporate ladder within the Herald-Republic, though rarely earning praise or hefty pay raises from his father. It wasn't the Colonel's style. He led by example. The Colonel had a tough exterior and was resolute in his convictions, a father who wanted to instill in his son an ethic of hard work and high expectations.

When the Colonel died in 1938 following a short illness, Ted realized his father had left more behind than just a flourishing newspaper. He had passed along sound advice, a road map with which to guide his life.

"Ownership of the only daily newspaper in a community carries with it a tremendous responsibility and obligation that must never be overlooked by those in control," Ted wrote of his father's beliefs. "A newspaper possesses great power to build and to make dreams come true or to totally disrupt and destroy. It must never be used for the personal gains or whims of its owner."

Ted may have traveled around the world, but I would like to think Yakima was always his most favorite place. The Colonel made sure of that.

# Ex-reporter offers peek into days gone past

*September 5, 1999*

L ove never crosses the path of a cop reporter.

That's something I always thought was true until I met Norm Collins. All too often our profession keeps the cop reporter on late-night shifts and in close proximity to shadowy convicts and grim-faced coroners.

Not for Norm. He had the time of his life. But then again he's not your typical cop reporter. In fact, the only record of his reporting is buried deep in our microfilm files. Even our human resources department couldn't find evidence of Norm ever working here.

That's understandable, though. He clocked into work 79 years ago.

I got a chance to sit down with Norm earlier this summer when he made a return trip to Yakima to rekindle fond memories of the days when he called Yakima his home and would chase after fires and take off from the Yakima airport in flimsy single-prop planes, soaring high above the Valley's verdant apple orchards.

The years have limited Norm's mobility. At 97, he has difficulty keeping his balance. His hearing is not what it once was, so during our conversation hand gestures and loud explanations filled in the gaps.

His eyes, though, sparkled whenever he spoke of his days as a reporter here and still had a strong grip, tightening his hand over my forearm whenever he wanted to emphasize a point he was making. His fondness for detail painted a remarkably clear picture of the past, as if you could close your eyes and see his life unfold, a documentary of sorts showing what Yakima was like nearly eight decades ago.

A busy street scene in downtown Yakima during the 1920s.
Photo courtesy of Yakima Valley Museum

Let's then turn back to September 20, 1920, when Prohibition is the rage and Woodrow Wilson still lays claim to the White House, to the streets of downtown Yakima where only a few months earlier the grandly opulent Mercy Theatre had opened. We see a lean confident-looking Norm Collins, 18 years old, his thick dark hair swept back to reveal a handsome face framed by a wide, toothy grin. He strides across Second Street and into the offices of Yakima's publishing empire where W.W. Robertson — better known as "The Colonel" — holds sway as publisher of both the Yakima Morning Herald and the Yakima Daily Republic.

Norm had arrived in Yakima hungry and looking for work. He had been on his way across the state, heading from Yellowstone to Seattle, when he made a sudden, unexpected detour. The reason was simple, Norm admits. He was broke. He figured, though, his situation was not so bleak. Having taken several journalism courses, he hoped the profession could be his meal ticket in the burgeoning fruit capital of Yakima.

It turns out Norm had no ordinary job interview that day. He stood face to face with none other than S.I. Anthon, one of the Northwest's most famous journalists. Colleagues and friends simply knew her as Sis. She had started out as a reporter in 1914 and would eventually work 52 years for the Yakima dailies until 1966, when she would die after being struck by a car while crossing Yakima Avenue on the way to her office.

At the time Norm met her, she was serving as a news editor.

Timing proved to be Norm's greatest ally. The Washington State Fair, which later became known as the Central Washington State Fair, had just begun its six-day extravaganza at the county fairgrounds and Sis was panic-stricken over who was going to cover the annual event. Apparently one of her veteran reporters was not up to the task that day after having quaffed one too many shots of illicit booze the night before. This apparently was not the first time this reporter had excused himself from work.

Sizing up the teenager standing before her, Miss Anthon decided it was an opportune time to make a personnel change. Norm got the job immediately, and the veteran reporter got canned.

Norm happily covered the fair, which ended up not only with a record attendance of 64,295 people but also a record number of hogs, a fact that the Yakima Morning Herald happily reported on its front page right next to a news story about the League of Nations.

Serving as police reporter allowed Norm the chance to snare breaking news stories, too. Like the time the first passenger plane arrived at the Yakima airport. Besides Norm showing up for its arrival, the plane's landing brought out a young couple that wanted to get married in mid-air. That made great news back then. It also allowed Norm a chance to take a ride himself in the open-cockpit airplane. The episode ended with a series of loop-the-loops that left Norm dazzled and dazed.

"It scared me to death," he confessed.

On land, Norm also proved prone to unexpected twists and turns. One of his most memorable news stories, in fact, almost claimed Norm as a Page One obituary.

As was his custom, Norm was hanging around the fire hall one day when an alarm sounded. The chief bolted to his car and told Norm to climb aboard. He did, clinging precariously onto the tail bumper. As the car careened over the railroad tracks, Norm lost his grip and tumbled headlong onto a busy Yakima Avenue. How he missed getting run over by the melee of fire trucks and other assorted piston-driven vehicles amazes Norm to this day. He finally came to rest in the gutter, from which the mayor of Yakima lifted him up and hauled his bruised and battered body to the nearest hospital.

That's one story Norm never wrote.

His police beat also took him up and down the Yakima Valley. To cover this route, often over tortuous dirt roads, Norm secured the loan of a motorcycle. But it was no ordinary two-wheeled bike. It was an Indian motorcycle, the kind that collectors nowadays will pay thousands for.

On his way through the Lower Valley, he always would stop by Toppenish and check in with the head boss of the U&I sugar plant. It was a big operation back then, fed by sugar beet farms that dotted much of Central Washington.

One day he arrived at the plant without his motorcycle. A friend of his, an actor on Broadway in New York City, had arrived for a short visit and loaned him his fancy new car for the daily trek to Toppenish and beyond.

While chatting with the plant manager, an attractive young lady strolled into the office. Her name was Vera and she was the boss's daughter. Stunned by her beauty, Norm did what any hot-blooded, bedazzled young man would do — he asked her to take a ride in his fancy new car.

Vera must have been suitably impressed, for a few years later, she married Norm and the two lived in what he called "marital bliss" for the next 73 years. Vera died earlier this year. She was 95.

Norm lasted only a year as Yakima's police reporter. He decided the advertising department was where he should be if he wanted to make some real money.

And that again proved heaven-sent for him — one of his advertising accounts, a breeder of chickens in Prosser, had failed to pay his bill. In lieu of payment, Norm accepted breeding stock.

The feathery chicks were very good to Norm, who was then living in the Seattle area. Under his watchful eye, the chickens merrily multiplied into what later would become the Washington Breeders Hatchery. The poultry even survived a move to Hawaii where he and Vera, along with their three children, lived for more than 20 years before returning to Lynnwood and the family estate.

Quite a nice little life for Norm Collins. Imagine how different it would have been if he hadn't come up short of cash that fall day in 1920 and had not asked a woman named "Sis" for a job and had never driven his friend's car to Toppenish and met a young lady named Vera.

What an unremarkable life it would have been.

# Fruit picker flies high to book his first million

*April 1, 2001*

A few weeks ago, Max Miller strolled into the airport terminal in Orlando, Florida.

He had no intention of leaving the terminal and joining the throngs of more than 35 million tourists who visit Walt Disney World and the Magic Kingdom each year. He didn't care about seeing the killer whales at Sea World, either.

The only thing Max had in mind was to stay the night at the airport and head back home to Yakima the next day.

Let's face it. Max is not your typical tourist. To him, it's pure mathematics. The more trips you take, the more miles you rack up.

And that's what Orlando was all about. So were the five trips to Munich he once piled up over a three-weekend span and the two back-to-back solo around-the-world trips he took two years ago when he was 75. Max delights in the thrill of feeling his internal odometer flipping over the numbers, wildly in rhythm, perhaps, to his own heartbeat.

Yes, Max is on a mission. The "tramp," as he refers to himself, is now in this game of life strictly for the miles, the kind of stuff you add up until, one day, there are six zeroes strung together that spell a million.

Those miles do come with their privileges. Nestled securely in his wallet is a "Premier Executive 1k Mileage Plus Gold" card from United Airlines, given to those who travel 100,000 miles, a distance he has long since eclipsed. With that United card and his Mileage Plus coupons, he has never had to travel in coach, always upgrading to business class or first class.

And his destinations are always exotic: London, Paris, Singapore, Melbourne and the outback of Australia, the Great Wall of China, the Alps in Switzerland, and the financial center of the universe: Hong Kong in the Orient.

For Max, though, these are only layovers on a much bigger trip. The final destination? One million miles.

A month ago, Max had flown an impressive 748,238 paid miles on United Airlines. Doris, his wife of 52 years, trailed a distant second with 541,719 miles. (Well, someone has to clean the house, right?). Max expects to reach the million mark next year, and might even eclipse it later this year if he can cram in enough trips like his recent one nighter to Orlando.

Max started his quest for the million-mile mark in 1983 when he went to England and Scotland. That was followed by a two-week tour of Switzerland, Munich, Rome and Venice.

Max is more accustomed to the one-night stand. This nomadic traveling has left Max with an impressive catalogue of repeat performances. He has flown to Hawaii 11 times, and an equal number of times to England, though Doris rarely goes since she dislikes its cold, wet climate. Instead, she prefers the steamy heat of Singapore, where they have made four treks, the most recent just a month ago. They have also taken family photos atop the Great Wall of China twice.

Last year alone, Max took to the airways 26 times, evenly divided between overseas junkets and trips within the United States. When pressed about this urge to see the world through the puny portal of a Boeing 757, Max simply shrugs his shoulders and says, in a calm, clipped, almost flat monotone: "I just like to travel." A lot.

As for gaining great insights into the human condition from all his travels, Max again keeps his pronouncements short, succinct and unambiguous.

"I think the more you travel, the more you appreciate the United States and what it means to be a citizen of this country."

When talking with Max, you don't get any zingers destined for the front page of London's Daily Mirror. What you get is Max, a fruit picker who has roamed the orchards of the Yakima Valley for nearly four decades, making friends and business contacts along the way, as well as a steady income. Whether it meant working 45 days straight picking Reds and Goldens or salvaging demolished buildings for scrap material as he once did when the Miller Building in downtown Yakima came tumbling down. He even sold discarded fruit and hand-pressed cider at a roadside stand. Max is resourceful, even to the extent of fashioning together several discarded motel units to serve as the family home.

Somehow Max has found a way to live beyond what you would assume a fruit picker's life would be. He has amassed an impressive collection of antique Model A's and T's, including a stunningly brilliant yellow 1930 Model A Ford coupe, which he keeps hidden in huge storage sheds behind his house. He also has a '31 Chevy and, not one, but two 1939 De Sotos, along with a 1963 Dodge Dart and two motor homes.

Perhaps the most impressive of the collection is his 1917 Ford speedster that has graced a number of parades in Yakima over the years and once appeared on the front page of the Yakima Herald-Republic, with both Max and Doris smartly attired and waving to a crowd of onlookers.

Max has even made a name for himself among the horticultural set by growing alongside the southern edge of his house corn that reaches astonishing heights. Each year, he's a cinch to capture top prize for "the tallest corn stalk" at the Central Washington State Fair.

Yes, when Max enters the United Airlines record books as a million-miler, he will surely be the first fruit picker to do so. Unlike other world travelers with gaudy mansions to their name, Max is no captain of industry or one who dines in five-star restaurants or sips Dom Perignon from a fluted glass.

He's a fruit picker who doesn't countenance such frills. He dashes in and out of inexpensive hotels and dines on the most American of all dishes — a quarter pounder served at McDonald's.

Don't expect, though, Max to celebrate his million-mile mark under McDonald's golden arches. He will be in the air, no doubt.

For Max, living doesn't happen along the margins, on the landings and takeoffs. It happens at 33,000 feet.

FOOTNOTE: *The indefatigable Max Miller reached the one-million-mile mark a year after I wrote this column. On April 10, 2002, Max eclipsed the milestone on a flight to one of his favorite spots — Orlando, home of Disney World. During that year when his Mileage Plus odometer flipped past 1,000,000 miles, he traveled to Singapore four times, California twice, one more flight to Orlando and, on one day alone, visited Seattle three times.*

# Black community needs new leadership

*January 30, 1994*

Although the words were written 17 years ago in the Yakima Herald-Republic, they still hold true today: "Approach Earl Lee with caution." A self-proclaimed black activist, Lee has gone out of his way in recent weeks to speak with news reporters about the sad and sorry state of race relations in this city.

Lee has focused on a confrontation involving Yakima police officers and Mel Stubblefield, a recognized leader in the black community and president of the Yakima Education Association, the largest teacher's union in Central Washington.

The uproar over the police stop on the night of Dec. 29 has led to several appearances by Stubblefield before the Yakima City Council and a public apology by the mayor and the police chief. Although the stop was legal, the manner in which several of the police officers conducted themselves was improper and rude, the police chief concluded after a lengthy review process. A disciplinary hearing has already been held for one of the officers and further training is planned for the department.

That hasn't satisfied Earl Lee. He's not a person who is willing to leave the final word with someone else.

Surely that must be the motivating factor behind Lee convening not one but two news conferences in recent weeks. He claims the news media gatherings were to corroborate and highlight what the Stubblefield incident had only hinted at — the presence of prejudice and racial discrimination within law enforcement agencies and the community as a whole.

When he called the newsroom to announce the news conferences, Lee promised he would "name names" and be precise in his accusations of police brutality and racial discrimination.

What he delivered, though, were bland generalities and a rambling diatribe about a community beset by obstinacy, ignorance and self-pride. Speaking from a prepared text, Lee quoted Edmund Burke, 18th century philosopher and orator, and invoked the names of Julius Caesar and Napoleon, not what you would call peace-loving souls. Despite failing to come forward with specific instances of police brutality that could be verified, Lee demanded the resignations of the Yakima County prosecutor, the Yakima police chief, several police officers and an attorney working for the Yakima School District. Each of the suggested resignations involves people with whom Lee has had confrontations.

He confided to all who would listen that he was seeking a federal probe of law enforcement officials, but refused to say which agency he would go to. That information, he professed, is confidential.

Just who is Earl Lee, and why should we care about what he says?

We do know a few things about him. Last year, a jury convicted the 38-year-old Lee of second-degree theft for accepting rent money and cash deposit for a home he did not own. Lee argued he had been negotiating to buy the home and that he had spent thousands of dollars repairing it when the owner backed out of the deal. He also claimed the charges brought by the prosecuting attorney were racially motivated. Lee has appealed the conviction.

As a fallout from the theft charges, and based on other unspecified reasons, the Yakima School District filed a letter of probable cause against Lee last spring and formally terminated his employment on June 30.

Lee has appealed the firing and a hearing is set for early next month.

There's more to Lee's past than a theft conviction and a lost job. In 1977, at the tender age of 23, Lee also claimed to be the kung fu champion of the world. In a feature story written by Herald-Republic reporter Patricia Wren, Lee is described as a lethal fighting machine, someone who should be approached with extreme caution.

"He is capable not only of fighting six Black Belts at a time, but he has been timed at throwing 60 punches in nine seconds."

Declaring Lee the world champ of kung fu, the story goes on to recount his travels to Europe, Canada, the Far East and throughout the U.S., countries where he claimed to have compiled an astounding record of 78 wins, no losses and no ties. After receiving the world cup trophy during ceremonies in Yakima, Lee said a United Artists director promptly signed him up for a major role in an upcoming movie expected to carry on the immense box-office appeal of the late Bruce Lee.

Yes, Earl Lee is too good to believe. Four days later, the Herald-Republic printed a lengthy story refuting everything that Lee had boldly asserted.

"Telephone calls to karate and kung fu experts in Seattle, Portland, San Francisco, Los Angeles, Toronto and New York failed to produce any evidence in support of Lee's claim," the reporter wrote.

Lee later admitted buying the world cup trophy locally.

So who is Earl Lee? He is no kung fu champ and no movie star; he has no fists of lethal power. Earl Lee is all of these.

And he's a talker, too. In one of his rare moments of insight, Lee said at his most recent news conference that Yakima has a very serious racial problem.

"These problems manifest themselves in the form of violence, racism, drug addiction, murders, gangs," he said. "To address these concerns appropriately, we need new people and new ideas, people who will accept the challenge, and are not tied to antiquated thinking and actions."

Few would disagree with this assessment. Yakima's black community needs to develop a new echelon of leaders to bring vitality and candor to the debate over race relations arising from such incidents as the Stubblefield police stop. New leaders with fresh voices must be welcomed, no matter how unsettling their message of change may be.

But don't look to Earl Lee to lead the way. He's too busy looking out for himself.

*FOOTNOTE: In the past two decades, Earl Lee has run numerous times for public office — Yakima City Council, school board and several times for a seat on the Yakima County commission. The perennial candidate has lost every race, often by sizable margins. In 2007, he appeared in a video posted by Yakima's KIMA-TV on its website carrying this provocative headline: "Past Political Candidate Turned*

*Deadbeat Renter?" The story detailed a dispute Lee had with a landlord, who said Lee owed him $20,000 in unpaid rent. Sheriff's deputies had to be called in to evict Lee from his garbage-strewn rental, the television station reported. Vowing to file a lawsuit seeking damages, Lee disputed the landlord's claim, referring to his detractor as both a liar and a crook.*

# For city manager, retirement is about finer things in life

*June 12, 2011*

Dick Zais has been called just about every name in the book during his nearly 33 years as Yakima's city manager: Darth Vader, Snidely Whiplash, King Richard. Critics have described him as humorless, cold and calculating.

Let's get real here. OK, Dick couldn't perform standup comedy at a nightclub in Seattle or Portland. But he can tell a joke or two. For the record, he's a great storyteller and can be quite engaging when he flashes a smile. He's the city's unofficial balladeer, a skilled raconteur delivering punch lines with ease. Who would have guessed?

Last month, on a Sunday afternoon filled with rain showers and brilliant sunshine, Dick entertained a large crowd with a detailed account — as only a city manager could — about his first date with Tammy Fellin, a former lobbyist with the Association of Washington Cities. The dinner date in Olympia came about thanks to the persistent efforts of then-Yakima mayor Mary Place, who happily played the role of matchmaker.

While driving to the restaurant, Dick lost his way. He asked Tammy to call and get directions. She did and relayed those to Dick. Always ready to debate the finer points of any issue, he told Tammy she couldn't possibly be right.

"Here, let me talk to the restaurant," Dick said.

Sure enough, he grabbed the phone and asked to hear the directions again. He quickly realized Tammy indeed was right.

Not a great way to start a date. So what to do now? Call the mayor for help?

Faced with impending doom, Dick did what any suitor would. He turned on the charm, and after the dinner plates had been removed, spent the better part of two hours talking with Tammy.

Now, some six years later, Dick found himself telling this light-hearted story inside the Yakima Area Arboretum. In his right hand he held a very large knife. That's funny, too, but this was also an immensely important time in his life and that of Tammy's. It was their wedding day.

A moment later Dick steadied his hand and cut the wedding cake, ending his story with a flourish and a round of applause. The married couple smiled.

You could tell it would be a great day at the very start of the wedding service when Tammy entered the crowded reception room (rain showers had forced the outdoor ceremonies inside). She appeared to be floating on air. How sweet, I thought.

That wasn't the case. Instead of being lifted on the wings of joy, Tammy arrived on the wheels of a scooter. She had broken a small bone in her foot a few days earlier. That required her to use an orthopedic scooter to support her injured leg. So with the help of the wheeled apparatus, equipped with handlebars, she glided into the room in near perfect rhythm with a tune being performed by a small string ensemble. Quite the entrance. Didn't expect to see that.

I also didn't expect to meet a group of guys who proudly called themselves the Whizzies. Wedding crashers? No, but what they did represent is another side of Dick that few outside of City Hall really know about.

The Whizzies date back more than 40 years when Dick attended the University of Washington. He never joined a fraternity and ended up living on campus in a dormitory. His dorm-mates assembled a flag football team, dubbed the Whizzies, and eventually earned the right to battle a fraternity house in the championship game. The frat guys had never lost in recent memory. It always ended up in a rout, with the Greeks pummeling the geeks.

But somehow the Whizzies prevailed, 16-13. Dick did his part. He claimed the role of water boy, slaking the thirst of the newly crowned gridiron gladiators, slayers of Greek row.

Ever since that fateful day, the Whizzies have gathered for reunions to recount their exploits on and off the flag football field. It seemed only fitting that they would assemble again to celebrate their water boy's wedding day. At one point, they even tried to disrupt Dick's storytelling by standing outside a window overlooking the cake-cutting ceremony and making funny faces. They failed to distract Dick, but we laughed nonetheless.

The Whizzies will return again on June 25 when the city holds a retirement party for its 61-year-old city manager at the Yakima Convention Center. They will join a long list of speakers that includes Dick's daughter, Eleanor; Fred Andrews, former city attorney, who spoke at the wedding; and his longtime friend and confidante, Richard Ostrander, former director of Yakima Valley Libraries.

No doubt, most of the speeches will recount Dick's prodigious skills as a city manager. He really has no equal when it comes to his mastery of budgeting.

A life well lived, though, is more than the sum of hours spent behind a desk. It's not quantity of work but quality of life that matters, and I'm not speaking about a fancy home or a lucrative retirement account. It's about the time you spend with those you love.

Dick was reminded of this message the hard way when a serious infection earlier this year nearly claimed his life. His lungs filled up with so many blood clots he could hardly breathe. The pain was excruciating. When a doctor studied his lung X-rays, he later told Dick they looked like those of a dead man.

That's why it was so sublime to hear Dick, the ultimate professional, tell a room filled with family, fellow workers and friends — yes, even the Whizzies — words that matter so much in life to a woman who means so much to him now.

And I'm sure the next time he suddenly finds himself lost, he will know exactly whom to ask for directions. That's the part of the story he will never forget.

# He's lived the advice he gives: Dream big

*May 17, 2009*

D an Miller doesn't let his motorized scooter slow him down. He charges fearlessly ahead and has little time to see if anyone else is following. But they do. By the thousands.

The 72-year-old Miller is one of Yakima's worst-kept secrets. His inspirational speeches have graced mammoth convention centers and small gatherings held in cramped community rooms.

Since 1990, more than 750,000 have listened and laughed at Miller's homespun anecdotes. I got a chance to hear him for the first time last month when he spoke at a conference I helped to organize here in Yakima for parents of children with special needs.

His self-published book — "Living, Laughing and Loving Life!" — has sold more than 70,000 copies, all by word of mouth and by personal appeal. He often autographs it with this simple advice: "Dream Big."

Indeed he does.

Miller had it made when he was an 18-year-old. Physically fit from growing up in the farming community of Pateros, Washington, the handsome teen was a gifted athlete, excelling in basketball, football and baseball.

Miller couldn't wait for the next stage in life — to go to college and become a physical education teacher.

Then one day, in the summer of 1955 after his high school graduation, Miller came down with what he thought was the flu. Now getting sick is no fun, but back in the 1950s, for a teenager to become ill, that was cause for panic.

Dan Miller, always with a smile.

The culprit was polio, a virus that blocks messages to the nerves and causes paralysis and sometimes death. It had reached epidemic proportions and left in its wake the vivid images of children in wheelchairs and iron lung machines. By the summer of 1955, more than 60,000 had died and another 2 million had been disabled.

It was in that fateful year that Dr. Jonas Salk announced to the world he had developed a vaccine. But it took time for the Salk vaccine to reach small farming communities like Pateros, with its population of 700.

For Miller, it arrived three weeks too late.

Once able to hit jump shots from anywhere on the basketball court, Miller was paralyzed within a few days after falling ill. At this point, his life had all the makings of a tragic tale to be told later by an embittered man grieving for what could have been.

But not for Dan Miller. After nearly 15 months of physical rehabilitation, he refused to give up on his dream of attending college, and so that's exactly what he did. He later earned a master's degree from Eastern Washington University and became a teacher, a physical education specialist and a principal in Prosser and Leavenworth, with several statewide awards to his credit.

Miller wanted to marry and raise a family. Those dreams came true, too. He and Judy, whom he met at college, will celebrate their 50th anniversary in August. They have three children and eight grandchildren.

The man with a paralyzed arm also dreamed of flying a plane and getting a pilot's license, and he accomplished those, too. He had to sit in the passenger's seat on the right side of the cockpit so he could work the controls with his left arm, but he succeeded. He even flew an ultralight, landing the flimsy aircraft in plowed fields and on dirt roads.

Oh, did I forget to mention the guitar? He wanted to play that, too. And be in a band, which he did for six years in his 20s.

Miller always dreamed big, and in his speeches and in his book, that's what he asks others to do as well. He certainly never gave up his desire to be a physical education teacher after polio had struck and turned the mere act of walking into a series of comedic pratfalls.

Then imagine yourself sitting across from your college adviser insisting that you want to become a gym teacher even though you could no longer run or jump, climb a rope or do a push-up. With his crutches at his side, Miller faced his adviser with his future hanging in the balance. Though the professor didn't know it at the time, he would become one of many dream makers in Miller's life.

"Well, let's see what you can do," the adviser said with a smile.

What a refreshing way to look at life. It's liberating, really. It certainly freed Dan Miller from the imprisonment that polio had placed on him. He knew all too well what he couldn't do. It was more important to be encouraged for what he could do.

And that was to dream big. Really big.

*FOOTNOTE: A year after Dan Miller appeared at the Fathers Network confer-ence, he retired from making speeches. In a span of 20 years, Dan delivered more than 1,500 presentations, speaking 107 times in his hometown of Yakima. He sold or gave away more than 72,000 self-published copies of his book from out of his garage. Dan has since moved across the mountains to LaConner, Washington, to be near his family. Despite being unable to walk due to Post Polio Syndrome, Dan says he gets around town just fine in his "Jazzy" power chair.*

# Like crime, the state sometimes doesn't pay

*January 30, 2000*

Tracy Lansden has learned his lesson.

"It teaches me in this town and county if you see crime, turn your back and run," Tracy said one morning while munching on French toast and watching the Jerry Springer television show.

Tracy has no desire to be called a hero or even a Good Samaritan. He would just like to get $600 so he can pay for the trip to the hospital and the stitches that got sewn into his skull. That's not asking much, considering he put his body — and in essence, his life — on the line to stop a thief.

The state, though, sees the matter differently. Officials think it's his fault that he got bonked on the noggin.

Let's not get ahead of ourselves. First, I should set the crime scene.

Tracy, a 36-year-old construction worker, had stopped by Top Foods to pick up a few ingredients to make shrimp salad. It was a little past midnight on Thanksgiving Day. He strolled over to the checkout stand and waited his turn.

Ahead of him was a guy who had plunked down on the counter one of the largest frozen turkeys Tracy had ever seen. The woman behind the cash register rung up $34 for the bird. This "big fella," as Tracy described him, seemed oddly dressed even for somebody on a midnight jaunt to the grocery store. He wore colored eyeglasses and had on a Jamaican hat atop what seemed to be fake hair that hung down in straight stringy strands. The man's loose fitting jogging suit concealed another set of clothes underneath.

The man leaned over and whispered something to the sales clerk. Tracy assumed the man didn't have enough money to pay for the frozen Butterball. Although he could only pick up a few words here and there, Tracy clearly heard "gun" and "robbery."

When you're in a store at midnight and the guy saying "gun" has fake hair and a weird hat atop his head, you assume the worst. That's when Tracy did something most other people wouldn't have done. He got curious and stepped forward.

"I guess I'm stupid," he confessed.

The clerk opened up the cash register and the man shoved her out of the way. When the crook grabbed the till and headed toward the exit, Tracy didn't hesitate. He ran after him.

At Top Foods, the exit is blocked by two automatic doors that are separated by 50 or so feet. That's where Tracy tackled the big fella. Although Tracy stands only 5 feet 8, he tips the scales at an imposing 240 pounds. So when Tracy got on top of the man, he felt confident the thief wasn't going anywhere.

Somehow, though, the man freed one of his arms and lifted the heavy till high in the air and smashed it against Tracy's head. Blood spurted out. But, as Tracy admits, he's hard-headed. The cash register drawer broke and splintered to the ground, and so did the crook's hope of fleeing the store.

For Tracy, it seemed like an eternity before store clerks, who were stocking shelves in the back of the building, arrived to lend a helping hand or, as in the case of one clerk, a ready foot that repeatedly found a resting place in the miscreant's private parts.

When the police showed up along with a medic, Tracy's first reaction was to go home and slap a towel around his head to staunch the bleeding. But the medic and the police told him to stop by the hospital and get a few stitches. Tracy was assured the state would pay for the treatment.

And so he did just that. Tracy went to Providence Yakima Medical Center and got his head stitched up. The price tag was nearly $600. He gave the hospital the case number he had gotten from the police, and went back to his home in Union Gap to enjoy his Thanksgiving with his family.

For Tracy, though, the satisfaction that comes with being a Good Samaritan didn't last long. Tracy received in the mail a letter — it was sent two days before Christmas — from a case manager with the Department of Labor and Industries, a state agency that oversees the Crime Victims Compensation Program.

"I am unable to allow your claim," the letter began.

The state agency described Tracy's actions at Top Foods accurately enough. But then came the clincher.

"The crime he committed was not against you but the store," the case manager wrote.

Since Tracy got whacked with the cash drawer after he had tackled the criminal, he didn't qualify for state coverage.

"The Crime Victims program does not allow claims when a person's action contributes to the injury that occurred to them."

So it turns out that Tracy's attempt to be a Good Samaritan was his ultimate undoing. In the eyes of L&I, he had "consented" to go after the criminal and, in so doing, "incited" the robber to split open his head, spilling blood over his coat and shirt and forcing an emergency room doctor to sew stitches into his traumatized skull.

"Since you were not a store employee, security guard or law enforcement officer you would not be expected to apprehend a criminal in Top Foods," the state concluded.

Unless Tracy appeals the decision in writing by the end of March, the matter will be closed. In Tracy's mind, it already is. What's the point of filing an appeal, he asks.

It's not as if the Crime Victims program is short of cash. In the current two-year budget, lawmakers set aside $25 million to pay for medical and health expenses, replace lost wages and cover pensions for victims of crime.

Tracy wants to make it clear he's not looking for any handouts. Although he's been in and out of work this winter, Tracy has no desire to be on the state dole.

"I never want to be on welfare," the manual laborer said. He would rather pay off the hospital bill in small installments, maybe five or 10 dollars a month. But it will be paid off, Tracy insists.

"I'm going to pay it," he said. "That's plain and simple."

Help may be on the way from several other sources. Tracy said Top Foods has contacted its insurance carrier to see if his medical bills could be covered under its corporate policy. The grocery store chain has already slipped him a $25 gift certificate.

The Yakima County Prosecutor's office has also stepped in. First, Deputy Prosecutor Tim Cotterell got the 26-year-old criminal, Harry Truman Hicks, to plead guilty to a charge of first-degree robbery. He then set up an account in Tracy's name to help cover his expenses.

Tracy's not spending the money just yet. "Give 'Em Hell" Hicks has to cool his heels for four years in prison before he can start paying back for the failed Thanksgiving Day heist.

Obviously, the state has let Tracy Lansden down. True, no one asked him to fling himself on Harry Truman Hicks, but when he did, something more should have been done than simply telling him: "Sorry, you don't fit our definition of a victim."

What good is a crime victims fund if you don't care for those injured in the line of duty, or in this case civic duty. That's a crime in itself.

# To B or not to B renamed for MLK

*March 5, 2006*

I magine renaming a street after the slain civil rights leader Martin Luther King Jr. and discovering there are no blacks living there.

Welcome to Yakima.

"I don't think so," confessed the Rev. Robert Trimble when asked if there were any black residents along B Street, a 17-block, one-way avenue in downtown Yakima that may soon be christened "Martin Luther King Jr. Boulevard."

Don't blame Trimble for this predicament. B Street was not his first choice. For 22 years, Trimble has found nothing but dead ends and lame excuses for why the city wouldn't rename a street after the Nobel Prize laureate.

Back in 1984, Trimble made his first attempt to name a roadway after Martin Luther King. It was Sixth Street, which passed through the heart of the city's historic black community, including the Bethel African Methodist Episcopal Church and the late Rev. Joe T. Denman's Greater Faith Baptist Church.

The request, though, met with angry words as a yelling match erupted when a city councilman referred to Trimble as an outsider, a modern-day carpetbagger, because he lived at that time beyond the city limits in Terrace Heights. Trimble was told to take his request elsewhere, to the county, which was powerless to act.

The council then offered what it considered an adequate substitute. It renamed a seldom-used park in southeast Yakima, at South Eighth and Beech streets, after Martin Luther King.

Trimble didn't think much of the trade-off.

"I came in asking for a Cadillac and I get a Volkswagen."

The council assumed it had seen the last of Trimble. But Trimble, who grew up in Atlanta and knew firsthand the struggles of blacks to gain their freedoms in America, wasn't about to give up.

And bless his heart, he didn't.

Now he is only hours away from realizing his dream. On Tuesday night at 7, in a special session at the Yakima Convention Center, the City Council will take up the issue of renaming B Street. With all seven members newly elected in the past two years, the council appears ready to make amends for the way it has treated Trimble and his backers in the past. Mayor Dave Edler, who's also a minister, said as much when he spoke in January at a citywide church service honoring Martin Luther King.

The Rev. Robert Trimble speaks at the dedication ceremony.

Trimble expects to bring more than 50 supporters to Tuesday's meeting. He doesn't want to take any chances. The pastor of Mount Hope Baptist Church in Yakima knows you can never take anything for granted when trying to pay homage to the controversial leader of America's civil rights movement.

Across the nation, nearly 700 streets honor Martin Luther King Jr. Surely one of the most famous is 125th Street in Harlem, which runs past the site of the famed Cotton Club where Duke Ellington once played and the Apollo Theater, hallowed ground for black performers seeking fame and fans.

In their book "Along Martin Luther King," published in 2003, author Jonathan Tilove and photographer Michael Falco crisscrossed America, exploring the streets and boulevards named after King, from Belle Glade, Florida, to Portland, Oregon. What they found was something more than a name stamped on a metal sign.

"There is a road that winds its way through the heart and soul of black America," wrote Tilove. "It may be called a boulevard, a drive, an avenue, a street, or a way, but it is always named Martin Luther King. It happened without grand design but with profound, if unrecognized, consequences. ... Map them and you map a nation within a nation, a place where white America seldom goes and black America can be itself. It is a parallel universe with a different center of gravity and distinctive sensibilities. ... There is no other street like it."

I'm sure Tilove would be amused by Yakima's B Street. It's certainly unlike any that he had come across.

When strolling down the 1.4-mile street on Wednesday, I did discover one thing. It's a hard street to love. The west-to-east street does have a few landmarks. City Hall, the county courthouse and, of course, that white monstrosity we call a jail.

Only a few businesses — the 103-year-old Helliesen Lumber, Yakima Rubber Stamp Works and Ofelia's Unisex Styling Salon — dare to have a street address on B. Most are like our newspaper building on North Fourth Street, offering a nondescript wall and a locked door leading to the sidewalk.

And then there are the parking lots, all 10 of them. Who says Yakima has a parking problem? Not on B Street.

The three-lane road does have its quirky charm, though. Take the home at the corner of North Ninth Street. On the chain-link fence surrounding the two-story house, a small hand-drawn billboard advertises the sale of whitefish flies, night crawlers and live maggots for only $1.25. I doubt MLK boulevards elsewhere in the nation can boast such a piece of Americana.

Let's face it, though. The street doesn't generate any warmth, any sense of community. It's all brick, concrete, a few boarded-up homes and little humanity to wander its sidewalks. But it's safe, and it's short.

So when the council seals the deal as expected, a celebration is called for, if for nothing else, to breathe a sigh of relief.

Perhaps a ribbon-cutting or a parade should be held. Trimble thinks April 4 would be a good spot on the calendar. It's the date Martin Luther King was mortally wounded by an assassin's bullet as he stepped out of Room 306 at the Lorraine Motel in Memphis, Tennessee.

It will be a bittersweet celebration, not only for Trimble, but also for one of the city's most revered black residents. He's Henry Beauchamp, and he was on the council back in 1984 when Trimble made his first pitch for renaming a street. Beauchamp could not stop a majority of five other council members from thwarting that dream. But now he, too, may be able to celebrate a decision that should have been made more than two decades ago.

Though he doesn't live there, Beauchamp is also one of the 183 property owners along B Street. That means he will soon be able to stand on the lot he owns and look over to a shiny new street sign, smile and say to himself, as so many others will: "Welcome home, Martin. Welcome home."

*FOOTNOTE: The Yakima City Council did indeed vote to name B Street for the celebrated civil rights leader, and the Rev. Robert Trimble finally got a chance to hold a citywide celebration. Loud applause followed the unveiling of the new sign, "Martin Luther King Jr. Blvd." Soon afterward, I stopped by the Mount Hope Baptist Church and gave Trimble my copy of "Along Martin Luther King." His story of persistence in the face of indifference certainly could have filled a chapter in that book.*

# Lighting a candle for those we loved

*Dec. 18, 2005*

Everybody is somebody to someone.

Those words kept running through my mind as I sat there and watched as mothers, fathers, aunts, sisters and grandchildren passed along a slender candle and recited this simple phrase: "I light this candle in memory of ..."

Then they called out the names of those who are no longer here: their son who once played football, their daughter who braided her golden hair, a niece who loved the chocolate chip cookies her aunt made and a grandson who placed his tiny hand into granddad's rough-hewn palm, waiting for a hug that was always there. They have all died, but their names remain, as do the memories of their smiles, their laughter.

That's how families at The Compassionate Friends 23rd Annual Candlelighting Ceremony celebrated the holidays, not with fanfare, but with a tenderness that melted your heart. The ceremony at Bethlehem Lutheran Church in Yakima was for those families who have lost a child. Nearly 100 attended, including me. When I lit a candle, I recited the name of Jed, my 18-year-old son who died three years earlier from complications following a severe seizure.

When I returned to the newspaper office the next day, I sifted through the long list of obituaries we published during the past year. As I looked at the names, I was struck by how many I had known and by how often our paths had crossed, either for a news story or just out in the community, working on a food drive together or just taking a minute or two to share a cup of coffee.

None could be considered famous in today's culture where notoriety is gauged by wealth and access to power. No, they are best known for what they did, in their distinct way, to leave our Yakima Valley a better place to live in.

## Jerry Henderson

He was Santa Claus incarnate.

Oh, how he loved to play Saint Nick. For nearly three decades, he would show up at Yakima Valley schools, always arriving in full costume, candy canes clutched in one hand and a bag of toys in the other. Kids flocked to see him, as if he were a rock star. Several times he arrived at Hoover Elementary School in a National Guard helicopter. If that's not rock stardom, I don't know what is.

His greatest delight, though, was being among children and adults with special needs. Through his volunteer work with the Yakima Kiwanis Club, Jerry helped to start the Aktion Club for adults with developmental delays. The club mirrors a regular Kiwanis Club with members being elected to office and overseeing meetings, which run off a strict agenda. Jerry was their leader, their commanding general. They followed him everywhere.

So at Jerry's memorial service at Englewood Christian Church, I wasn't surprised when the entire Aktion Club showed up and sat in the front pews, some 40 strong. When I asked those in attendance if they wanted to say something about Jerry, one of the Aktion Club members stood up and talked, slowly at first but then with great passion. After she sat down to loud applause, suddenly a score of hands shot up in the air. Nearly every Aktion Club member wanted to speak.

They loved Jerry, and they wanted everyone in the church, and our community, to know what he had meant to them.

## Norm Anderson

To those who knew him — and there were legions — he was called simply "Norm." He was an immensely likable man whom I first met while he served as a ranger in the Wenatchee National Forest.

After caring for our forests, he turned his attention to Camp Prime Time near Clear Lake where families of children with special health care needs and developmental delays are treated to a weekend of fun at no charge thanks to a cadre of volunteers who cook, clean and sing songs at night around a campfire.

He was the camp's caretaker. Always quick with a story that seemed to have no end, or at least none that you could figure out, Norm would often be found sitting, or rather rocking, on a chair in the camp's kitchen, dispensing tips on how to cook but never lifting a finger himself to carry out the tasks.

Sadly, there was no formal memorial service for Norm. He deserved one. I bet if there were one, it would still be going on, with each of his friends trying to top the other with a "Norm" story.

## Anne Veronica Finch Byerrum

A painting meant more to Anne than colors on canvas. It became a starting point for exploring the limits of creativity.

Through her work as the executive director of the Allied Arts Council and later as arts director for the Yakima School District, she made art the impetus for learning, igniting a child's imagination the way a sunflower captures a rainbow when painted in watercolors.

What impressed me most about Anne was the courage she displayed while fighting cancer. Often she could barely talk due to the ravages of her long stints of chemotherapy. She would speak, nonetheless, saying "hi" to her friends and, one memorable night, standing before hundreds of people at the Capitol Theatre to introduce best-selling author and advocate of spiritual healing, Dr. Bernie Siegel.

Yes, Siegel could inspire cancer patients to laugh in the face of their debilitating illness and draw strength from that very act of defiance. Anne took that message to heart and showed all of us you could also live with a splash of color, like the paintings she wonderfully drew.

———

Over the years, I continued to write short eulogies for those who left a mark in my life. It was my way of lighting a candle in their memory — with words.

———

*Dec. 17, 2006*

## Ron Krous

You don't get to pick your neighbors. Sometimes, you may never see them; other times, you wish you never would again.

When my family moved into our home on South 32nd Avenue years ago, we got lucky for one of our neighbors was Ron Krous.

He and Mary, his wife of 52 years, raised six children in a large two-story home on the corner lot at Tieton Drive and 32nd Avenue.

Our property was separated by a long line of tall pines, which reminded me of Robert Frost's famous poem, "Mending Wall," and this wonderful prose: "He is all pine and I am apple orchard."

Sadly, in my case, there were no apple trees filling my backyard. I had raspberry bushes, as did Ron.

But as Frost predicted, "Good fences make good neighbors." That was certainly the case with Ron and me. So next to the pines, at an opening where a tangle of concord grapes grew, we would stand and chat.

We would talk about whatever came to mind, mostly gardening. If we were really desperate, we would talk about work. Since Ron had been the director of engineering for KNDO-TV for four decades, we had a lot of material to pick through.

But the best part about chatting with Ron was his laughter. There are some people who are blessed with a laugh that instantly has everyone else laughing in harmony. Ron was one of those. And he wasn't stingy with it, either.

On June 27, I lost my neighbor and his laughter.

Late this fall, as I was raking up leaves that had fallen from my walnut tree, I stared at the small opening where we had talked and realized fences don't really make good neighbors. Good people do.

## Clayton Frazier

Just as airlines develop frequent fliers, daily newspapers seem to attract frequent callers. Clayton Frazier was one of those.

Though he taught science and biology, Clayton's claim to fame was in football where he coached Eisenhower High School to its only undefeated season and a state championship in 1964.

He ended coaching in 1970 and stopped teaching 12 years later. But Clayton never retired from his favorite activity — calling the Yakima Herald-Republic. Clayton had a knack for talking and a memory that wandered near and far. That meant a phone call from him guaranteed the listener at least 15 minutes on the phone.

While Clayton often would call the sports department, over time he began calling me. He was always considerate, asking how my family was doing and inquiring about the health of my wife, Bronnie, who was undergoing cancer treatment. After her death six years ago, one of the first calls I got when I returned to work was from Clayton. He sobbed as we talked that day.

But for some reason, I had never seen his face. That changed one fateful summer night.

While flipping through the channels in search of something better to watch than another Seattle Mariners loss, I came upon the sight of an older gentleman sitting on a chair with a stack of papers in his lap. He was belting out one song after another and he did it with such ferocity that I found myself transfixed.

His throaty voice was strident and whimsically off key. After finishing a song, he would sift through the stack of rumpled papers and begin again — a different tune, but with the same earsplitting result.

That's when it finally struck me. I know that voice. It belongs to Clayton Frazier.

When I later talked to Clayton about his frequent appearances on Yakima's public access station, he claimed the act of singing — regardless of its quality — was good for his health.

Thinking I wanted to hear more, Clayton later dropped off two cassette tapes of his musical repertoire. I took them home and promptly forgot about them — until Jan. 30, when I heard of Clayton's death.

That's when I searched through my file cabinet to make sure the tapes were still there.

They were.

I still haven't listened to them. One day I will. I might even sing along. I hear it's good for your health.

Doris Norris and I meet for the last time.

## Doris Norris

I don't have to go far to see my longtime colleague, Doris Norris. She's smiling at me from a photo in my cubicle. It was taken about this time last December when several of her friends took Doris out to lunch.

I invited myself since I was on my way to help hand out Christmas gifts at a nearby school. I arrived dressed in a rented elf costume. Doris didn't seem to mind, though. She had become accustomed to laughing at me, and I rarely disappointed her.

When I first met her, I was the one laughing. It was a natural reaction when anyone heard her name.

I met Doris 30 years ago when I began working as a cop reporter at the Skagit Valley Herald in Mount Vernon, Washington. By then, Doris had already made a name for herself as a columnist, writing under the provocative heading of "From a Woman's Point of View."

We parted company a few years later when she returned with her husband Jack to her native soil — the Yakima Valley.

But it seems Doris and I were meant to cross paths, over and over again.

In late 1982, I also headed over the mountains — and landed a job here as city editor, and guess who was there to greet me? Doris.

For the next decade, Doris worked across from me in the newsroom.

Doris had a sharp mind and a knack for being exquisitely candid, even when the truth was painful to take. She didn't tolerate fools lightly and that meant she had to tolerate a lot knowing me.

Which brings me back to that photo of us at the restaurant last year. It was the last time I saw Doris alive. Two months later at age 80, she died in Evanston, Illinois, where she had gone to live with one of her daughters.

What a coincidence. Evanston is the city where I was born. Our paths, for one last time, had crossed again.

*Jan. 2, 2011*

## Bob Clem

Last Sunday we lost one of Yakima's finest treasures.

He was a popular television and radio comedian, an impersonator and convention speaker without equal, a skilled artist in woodworking and a gifted raconteur who could weave stories together seamlessly, leaving listeners doubled over in laughter.

Though he also ran a successful advertising business and served as manager of the Yakima Air Terminal, Bob never took himself too seriously, nor others.

One of Bob's finer moments came when the city of Yakima was digging itself out of more than 600,000 tons of volcanic ash following the eruption of Mount St. Helens in 1980. Most of the ash ended up in what is now Chesterley Park. The city was looking for a savior, and to the rescue appeared Dr. Hana Claus, who claimed to be a famous research chemist and the inventor of a secret, unproven resin that could bind the gray ash and turn it into cash through the sale of such essentials as toilet bowls. When Claus promised hundreds of jobs and an expanded tax base, Yakima took the bait and offered to fund his venture to the tune of $50,000.

Bob knew a charlatan when he saw one. So when he heard Claus was holding a news conference to demonstrate the wonders of his unproven resin, Bob jumped into action. He rented a stretch limousine and showed up dressed in a furry bunny outfit wielding a Samurai sword and an aerosol can of fake resin. Claus was laughed out of town.

Bob, though, never impersonated who he was -- a devoted husband, father and friend. He had a heart of gold. Even while undergoing cancer treatment last fall, he took the time to send me a note, wishing me well on my retirement from the newspaper.

Though Bob could never resist a joke with a great punch line, he really never wanted to have the last laugh. He just wanted to be part of the laughter. That's not a bad quality to have. It doesn't hurt to be wearing a pair of floppy bunny ears, either.

## Mark Strosahl

It seemed only fitting that the memorial service for Mark Strosahl, held March 6, was at The Seasons Performance Hall, a nearly century-old domed church on Naches Avenue, which his family transformed from a sanctuary for meditation to one for soul-soaring music. Whether it was setting up sound systems for rock stars or performing in his band with his wife Lori, Mark was never far from a guitar pick or an amplifier.

My wife Leslie was a classmate of Mark's at Eisenhower High School in the late 1960s and always marveled at the brilliance of his mind. So did everyone else who came in contact with him.

I met Mark in 1983 shortly after I arrived at the Yakima Herald-Republic. Back then Mark was a guiding force at his parents' company, United Builders, and had been invited by the editorial board to discuss how the economy was faring in our area. Mark did that easily enough, but he also spoke with authority on what seemed an endless number of topics. I soon realized Mark was more than just a builder of homes; he was Yakima's very own Renaissance man, who could play a Sammy Hagar guitar riff one moment and the next be ready to discuss the finer points of Buddhism.

So it didn't seem odd when Mark left the construction business in 2002 to buy the venerable Greystone restaurant on Yakima's historic Front Street and pursue another one of his passions, cooking.

On June 19, 2009, Leslie and I joined another couple at the Greystone for a special dinner we had won at an auction. It turned out to be the same day Mark learned he had leukemia, a disease that would claim his life eight months later. Despite the grim diagnosis, Mark and Lori greeted us with open arms.

When we asked about the Kobe beef on the menu, Mark spent the next 10 minutes describing in exquisite detail the cut of chuck roast we would be served. It was as eloquent a speech on the creative art of cooking as I have heard. Or ever will.

Leslie and I picked the beef. It was as good, if not better, than what Mark had explained. That's what you came to expect from Mark — a brilliant mind always at work.

## Julie Gray

Nine months later, on Nov. 20, it seemed only natural that the memorial service for Julie Gray would also be held at The Seasons. No, she wasn't related to Mark or the Strosahl family, but she dearly loved performing there with the Yakima Symphony Chorus.

Julie had a talent not only for singing but teaching as well, having taught creative writing and English for more than 18 years in Wyoming. Later, the 69-year-old served as Selah's city supervisor, greeting everyone who walked through City Hall with a smile so warm and genuine you couldn't resist saying "Hi."

Leslie and I first met Julie through her husband, Ronnie Gray, who played the drums and sang at Englewood Christian Church during its Sunday evening services. If the Yakima Valley held a vote for the most charming couple, Julie and Ronnie would win hands down.

With music so much a part of their lives, it made sense that Julie's memorial service would be filled with songs and drum rolls. In her final days, that's what Julie requested and that's what Ronnie delivered, a musical tribute without rival.

Guitars, music stands and drum sets were scattered across the front of the performance hall as we took our seats. Ronnie had brought together not one but three bands he had performed with over the years. During the service Ronnie moved from one drum set to the next, first playing a few songs with Margie and Her Sidekicks, a country western band from the Lower Valley. Then he moved over to play several Brazilian tunes with Yakima's KJC Jazz Company before jamming with the Royal REAC Jazz Band from the Tri-Cities.

At one point, several flute players held forth from the upper balcony. And yes, the Yakima Symphony Chorus was there, too, rising up from the church pews to perform "And the Glory of the Lord" from Handel's Messiah.

Near the end of the service, Ronnie sang, "What a Wonderful World," with each word bathed in warm honey.

Julie would have been proud of what Ronnie had done that day, a stirring testament to the joy for life they had shared together.


## Lance Braden

An hour after Julie's service had ended, another one began at the Capitol Theatre. The main floor filled quickly. Young boys and girls mingled with men and women in their 60s and 70s. Smiles mixed with tears. Friends hugged and lingered long in the embrace. It seemed that most of Yakima was there.

Lance died Nov. 14 after succumbing to the ravages of diabetes. Besides leaving behind his wife, Michele, and two children, Lance also left behind a legion of friends and countless admirers who found his boyish grin irresistible. I don't care if you were 8 or going on 80, Lance had a way of connecting. Just the sound of his voice, with all of its high-pitched peaks, could make a room full of unruly kids or grumpy adults come to life. He had the gift of gab and the heart to go with it.

I got to know Lance at the YMCA, where the young dynamo had worked his way up from a teen counselor at Camp Dudley to the Y's associate executive director. I served on the Camp Dudley committee with him when he oversaw the camp. He loved to see young kids explore the outdoors and learn how to accomplish goals they never imagined were possible. Thanks to Lance, my son with special needs was able to enjoy the Camp Dudley experience.

Lance tried his best to get a smile out of everyone, especially me. Once when I arrived at the YMCA for a meeting, he introduced me, in a voice far too loud for the task: "I'd like you to meet my Dad." I then spent the next five minutes explaining to everyone that I really wasn't his Dad. Lance, of course, didn't stop there. When I finally headed for the door an hour later, Lance called out after me: "Hey Dad, can I use the car tonight? Please?"

After about five or six of these "Meet my Dad" episodes, I finally gave up. So when Lance and I would arrive together at a meeting or event, I would greet others in a voice too loud for the setting: "I'd like you to meet my son."

I will miss those times. It's as if I have lost a son. I know I have surely lost a friend. So has everyone in the Yakima Valley.

Lance Braden and his Camp Dudley campers.

# Our friend, Martin

*January 12, 2012*

Even in the calm of a winter's afternoon, when I stare at the Oregon grape bushes in Martin Howell's front yard, I fear they're still growing. For years, Martin had let the bushes, along with Aspen trees, pine, spruce and laurel, to grow wild. Martin claimed he was a naturalist. Others argued he was a bit lazy or just plain ornery. Touch my tree, he told one neighbor, and I will call the city and complain about your garage that's built too close to my property line.

Unlike the dark, twisted bramble crowding his yard, Martin brought a rainbow of bright colors and a world of possibilities to those of us living in the Yakima Valley. He offered a shoulder to lean on in times of trouble and a hand to hold when death approached. Whether he was pushing a nonprofit organization through the rigorous process of figuring out where it was headed or talking to a stranger struggling through a tough divorce, you could count on Martin to be there.

Martin arrived in Yakima in 1991 with a master's degree in social work and used his skills as a gifted counselor to help groups forge alliances where none had existed before, lending support to a vast array of organizations including the Yakima YMCA, Yakima Valley Museum, American Red Cross, Yakima Valley Folklife Festival and the Humane Society.

He showed a knack for bringing together people of different means and backgrounds. Take, for instance, the "Not So Buff" group he formed at the

YMCA. He led this disparate group of stockbrokers and apple growers in exercises to improve not only their health but also their outlook on life.

And when it came to an unwanted dog or cat, he never turned his back. In Martin, they had a friend for life.

Martin Howell at home with his four-legged friends.

That's why his death last summer shocked the community. Not because it was so sudden. It was, but he had been near death several years earlier following a devastating illness. It's shocking because we can't imagine life without him, without his laughter, without his wit and candor that left you at times speechless, and more often in admiration, saying to yourself, "Now why didn't I think of that first?"

A month after Martin died, I showed up at his house with my wife, Leslie, to help clean up his yard so his house could be put on the market for sale. Norm Walker, Martin's close friend and a fellow counselor, warned us about the tangled vegetation. Still, we were not prepared for what greeted us. The term "curb appeal" did not apply here. Grass grew knee deep along the street where a row of bushes sported branches that had collapsed onto a lawn pockmarked with dead grass.

We persevered. Pruning shears and a crosscut saw in hand, I whacked away at several rhododendron and an Oregon grape bush that obscured the view of Martin's front porch. Often I would come upon a surprise — a small wooden birdhouse. I found six or seven. Apparently Martin couldn't resist a yard sale, and would return with boxes filled with birdhouses and other flotsam that he hoped his friends would find irresistible. That rarely happened. So Martin ended up with nearly everything he bought.

Yes, Martin was a hoarder, and that also meant collecting books. His house was cluttered with stacks of books, ranging from sociology to Sudoko. Among the volumes of prose was one of Martin's favorites: "Who Moved My Cheese? An Amazing Way to Deal with Change in Your Work and in Your Life," by Spencer Johnson. Martin urged me to read the international bestseller.

"You've got to," he told me one day, his voice rising with excitement at the thought of me flipping through the book.

I never did, until a few months after Martin's death. The quirky, 98-page book is loaded with simple but compelling messages. It's a parable about two mice, Sniff and Scurry, and two "littlepeople" named Hem and Haw. The foursome lives in a maze and struggle to find cheese to survive. Sniff and Scurry are quick to discover that their stockpile of cheese has dwindled and is starting to stink. The mice realize they need to change. So they go looking for new cheese.

"The quicker you let go of old cheese, the sooner you find new cheese," Johnson wrote, using the image of cheese to symbolize what we value in our lives or on the job. The maze represents the world in which we live.

Hem and Haw, as their names imply, stay put in the maze, waiting for cheese to come to them. Finally, Haw gets into action when he understands that he must adapt to survive. He soon overcomes his fears and heads off into the maze.

"Change happens when the pain of holding on becomes greater than the fear of letting go," Johnson wrote. He completed this thought with a provocative question: "What would you do if you weren't afraid?"

Johnson published his motivational book in 1998 after his life fell apart following a divorce. Johnson realized he couldn't expect a different outcome — of having a vibrant and lasting marriage — if he himself wasn't willing to change.

This message of personal change is something Martin spoke often about. So I doubt Martin would have been too upset about us clearing out his yard.

He would have understood. As Johnson wrote: "See what you're doing wrong, laugh at it, change and do better."

Now in a world without Martin, I miss his laughter. But that's always the case with people you care about. So you've got to supply the laughter yourself, as I did each time I pulled out a birdhouse from his Oregon grape bush. I laughed till I cried.

# Eat, Drink and then Drink Some More

*"You have to be always drunk. That's all there is to it — it's the only way. So as not to feel the horrible burden of time that breaks your back and bends you to the earth, you have to be continually drunk. But on what? Wine, poetry or virtue, as you wish. But be drunk."*
— CHARLES BAUDELAIRE, 19TH CENTURY FRENCH POET

# Taking Betty Crocker's brownies to a higher level

*March 7, 2014*

When the citizens of this fine state voted to make the sale of marijuana legal for recreational use, I doubt we fully considered the profound changes this decision could have on our once idyllic lives.

We have already witnessed what's taking place in Colorado when its marijuana law went into effect in January — long lines of wild-eyed, frantic buyers caught in the grip of skyrocketing costs and dwindling supplies.

Despite roadblocks against the sale of pot sweeping across many communities in Eastern Washington, our state's law is still expected to kick into low gear later this summer. And when it does, we may have much more to worry about than a gold-rush mentality among consumers eager to snatch up pot pedigrees named Jack the Ripper and Trainwreck. I'm talking about our obsession with cooking.

Instead of simmering a sweet mustard glaze for grilled salmon, we could be spending countless hours hunched over a saucepan slow cooking an oily mix of THC, the active chemical in pot. This cannabis concoction will inevitably find its way into hash browns, banana bread, mac 'n' cheese and, our most patriotic of desserts, apple pie.

A batch of brownies will also take on a whole new aroma. Who could have guessed our state's new marijuana law would return Betty Crocker to rockstar status and make her ultimate fudge brownie mix a best seller at Wray's supermarket.

Here's a case in point. Recently a well-respected member of the Yakima community decided to go where she had never gone before. Like President Clinton, she never inhaled weed during her youth when Timothy Leary, Harvard lecturer and LSD devotee, encouraged everyone to "tune in, turn on and drop out."

Times changed, and with them, this woman's attitude about pot. So last summer, a year after voters passed the initiative, she told her grown children what she wanted for her 70th birthday party — marijuana brownies. She asked them to go forth and score her a baggie of weed. Sadly, her offspring failed to bring Maryjane home for supper.

Undeterred by this, she headed out on her own and purchased the illicit drug on the streets of Yakima. When she parlayed the pot, the dealer even handed her a recipe for brownies.

The result? Marijuana brownies to die for. And no, contrary to what doomsayers of relaxed pot laws would argue, she didn't keel over. In fact, she said the enhanced dessert was pleasant to the tongue and to the electrons exploding excitedly in her brain. Yes, she got pleasantly high along with her children. How's that for family bonding?

I remember my first, and only, consumption of marijuana brownies. It took place in Cleveland, Ohio, back in 1970. I bit into a square of what looked like a brownie. I suddenly found myself gasping for air and picking out thin shreds of grass from between my teeth. Though the brownie had tested my gag reflexes, it did little to enhance my euphoria.

It appears dumping a cup of unrefined pot into a mixing bowl is not recommended. Thanks to the wonders of the Internet and the website the-weedblog.com, I came across what is touted as "The Perfect Weed Brownie Recipe." It requires flavorless cooking oil, brownie mix, a frying pan, a wooden spoon, a coffee filter, electric grinder, and the *pièce de résistance*, an ounce of dank — that's slang for very potent pot. And remember, it's now legal in this state to possess an ounce of pot.

The key is to extract the powerful THC from the grass and reduce it to a puddle of oil. To accomplish this, you must first pulverize the dank into powder, dump it into a frying pan with the oil and cook the potion on low heat for two to six hours.

After you have driven yourself stir-crazy staring at the frying pan for most of the day, pour the liquid through a coffee filter and blend the musky oil with the brownie mix. As Betty Crocker would then advise, "bake as directed."

Such is the brave new world awaiting us here in the Palm Springs of Washington. Let's don't forget, though, this altered state comes with a warning: "You are what you eat."

# Nice pairing: fine writing and fine wines

*April 4, 2014*

D ust rose up and enveloped the orange hood of my Datsun B-210 as I parked the car in front of a large outbuilding. In one hand I clutched a copy of Esquire magazine. Just then, another car pulled up. The driver stepped out into the afternoon sun and stared at me. He was also holding a copy of Esquire.

This stroke of serendipity in 1978 had less to do with divine intervention than it did with an abiding affection for Esquire. I had driven over from Mount Vernon while the other guy was from Seattle. We had both come across an article by Roy Andries de Groot, a well-respected food and wine writer who, after losing his sight during the blitz of London in 1940, decided to devote his life's work to writing about culinary masterpieces and exceptional wines. In Esquire, De Groot had declared to wine enthusiasts from France to California that Hinzerling Winery, nestled in the farming community of Prosser, was producing "world-class wines."

Curious to see what was inside, I entered the building. Instead of finding a tasting room with tables and comfy sofas, I felt I had walked into an auto repair shop. Rather than marble flooring, my shoes touched something less divine — a concrete slab.

Suddenly the room exploded with sunlight as Mike Wallace, Hinzerling's winemaker, made a dramatic entrance. He shook our hands and welcomed us with a warm smile. Seeing us gripping tightly to our copies of Esquire, Wallace figured we were another hapless pair of "wine nuts" from the westside. With a quick move, Wallace stepped over to an old, battered refrigerator and flipped open the door.

Mike Wallace, Washington's legendary winemaker.

Imagine my surprise when the refrigerator tilted crazily forward and jettisoned several bottles of the prized wine. Somehow my fellow wine taster and I were able to catch the bottles before they exploded on the unforgiving floor. We laughed at our good fortune and were soon treated to colorful tales by Wallace of his pioneering efforts at making wine in the Yakima Valley. As many others would happily discover over the years, Wallace is as renowned for his storytelling as he is for his wines.

While studying in the early 1970s at the University of Washington, Wallace had already set his sights on making wine in Prosser. But where to learn more about the craft of wine making? That led him to Dr. Walter Clore, widely regarded as the "father of Washington wine." At the time Clore was busily at work tending to varieties of European wine grapes at the

Washington State University experiment station in Prosser. Clore's advice to Wallace — head south to California and enroll in the wine program at U.C. Davis.

Wallace returned and began planting chardonnay, merlot and cabernet sauvignon north of Prosser in what is now the Kestrel View Estate Vineyard. According to the Great Northwest Wine website, these vines are some of the oldest in the state.

In 1976 Wallace uncorked his first bottle at Hinzerling Winery.

How De Groot discovered Hinzerling is, as they say, another vintage Wallace tale. It turns out a columnist with the Seattle Post-Intelligencer had become fascinated with the nascent wine industry in the Yakima Valley and arranged De Groot's trip a year after Wallace had opened Hinzerling.

Following a tour of the vineyards, Wallace treated the author of "Feasts for All Seasons" to dinner inside the winery's garage. Yes, no candelabra or white linens to honor Esquire's celebrated columnist. *Haute cuisine* may be fine for those dining along the Champs-Elysées in Paris, but not Hinzerling Road in Prosser.

Wallace described De Groot as an inquisitive and chatty guest, who didn't mind referring to himself as Baron de Groot.

"His stately presence, English accent and imperious manner perhaps contributed as much to his reputation as a man of taste, as his culinary expertise," the New York Times noted in his obituary on September 18, 1983. The 73-year-old De Groot died from a self-inflicted gunshot wound after becoming depressed due to failing health.

When talking to Wallace recently, I mentioned how De Groot and I had crossed paths again. After retiring four years ago, I tried out for a play at the Warehouse Theatre. Written by Yakima playwright Kurt Labberton, "Dinner/Music" revolved around a group of friends attempting to recreate a dinner party that Cole Porter, songwriter and fabled socialite, once hosted in 1947 for King Edward VIII and his American divorcee, Mrs. Wallis Simpson. The writer, who later lavishly described the feast, was none other than Roy Andries de Groot.

How's that for a wild coincidence, I told Wallace. We both laughed loudly, the same kind of outburst we shared 36 years ago when Wallace's world-class wines came tumbling out of his fridge.

# The perfect symbol of life — a fried onion ring

*June 30, 2011*

S o here's a spot quiz: What do the cities of Glenview, Atlanta, Walla Walla and Yakima have in common?

It has nothing to do with days of sunshine a year (Yakima has the most with 300) or the number of wineries (Glenview has zilch; Walla Walla has more than 100). And don't even think about a "strong mayor" form of government. Walla Walla doesn't have one and Yakima is still mulling it over.

Give up? Here are a few hints: It's a versatile vegetable that can be dunked in a vat of beer batter, fried in hot oil and delivered in fist-sized chunks requiring a steak knife to subdue.

It's none other than the succulent, guilt-ridden, calorie-cluttered fried onion ring. And really, with the Fourth of July only a few hours away, I can't think of a better way to celebrate the gastronomic richness of this nation than by reliving the joys of munching down on a hand-cut onion ring that's been washed in a bath of egg water, dusted with flour and submerged, ever so briefly, in a pot of sizzling oil, its skin turning a golden brown.

My first taste of fried onions came early in life. I could barely reach the table but that didn't stop my parents from shoveling a plateful within reach of my stubby fingers.

These were no pedestrian onion rings, either. Served up at Hackney's on Harms in the Chicago suburb of Glenview, they have been consistently ranked by experts as some of the best in the U.S.

Opening in 1939, Hackney's has stuck to its menu of thick, juicy hamburgers on dark rye bread. The fried onion rings are equally as popular with up to 400 pounds being served daily during the summer.

And they don't come out in a puny plastic basket. They arrive as a thicket of thinly sliced sweet Spanish onions formed into the shape of a small loaf of bread. It's quite a sight. For me, a 7-year-old at the time, it bordered on a religious experience.

Later in my early 30s, I had the good fortune of traveling to Atlanta where I visited a friend. He insisted on taking me to the city's famous Varsity Drive-In. What an institution. Each day, some 10,000 customers pour more than 300 gallons of chili over enough hot dogs that, if lined up end to end, would stretch for two miles.

I decided on a chilidog served with a line of mustard running down its center — what the locals call a Yankee dog because of its yellow streak. No hard feelings about the Civil War, right? Then came the onion rings, cooked to perfection and tossed into a cardboard boat. The website Roadfood.com gives these O-rings a five-star rating.

While onions date back to 5000 B.C., fried onion rings in the U.S. are a fairly recent fascination, reportedly making their first appearance at the Pig Stand restaurant chain in Oak Cliff, Texas, in the early 1920s. It appears the Pig Stand also lays claim to Texas toast, an honor of dubious distinction.

Though far from Texas, the fried onion rings at the Whitehouse-Crawford Restaurant in downtown Walla Walla may hold the distinction of being the most exquisitely carved in the country.

Housed in a brick building that once did double duty as a lumber-planing mill and furniture factory, the gourmet restaurant boasts a menu with such offerings as Wagyu beef tenderloin steak simmered in red wine and topped by mushrooms sauteed in *foie gras* butter.

But nothing quite compares to its servings of Walla Walla sweet onions, which are dusted in flour and seasoned with a jolt of cayenne pepper. The frying process is so gentle that the thin strands of onion appear to be suspended in air when they arrive at your table.

Just as the Whitehouse-Crawford is steeped in history with its turn-of-the-century building, so too is Gasperetti's Restaurant and its claim to the onion-ring hall of fame. Mario Gasperetti first introduced his tasty deep-fried appetizer in 1949 at his restaurant in Union Gap. He got the recipe from a

Frenchman, who was working in Mario's kitchen at the time. He passed along the highly prized list of ingredients with one stipulation — that Mario could never divulge the recipe to anyone else.

Mario kept his word and so too has his son, John, who reopened Gasperetti's with his mother, Minnie, in 1966 at its present Yakima site at 1013 N. First St.

"If I tell you the ingredients, I would have to kill you," joked John as I tried to pry the information from him last week. His longtime chef, Brad Patterson, also refused to budge.

For a time, John even refused to list the onion rings on his menu. Reports of the tantalizing rings were passed along only by word of mouth.

No problem there. In fact, that's how I first heard about Gasperetti's nearly 30 years ago while preparing to move my family from Mount Vernon. After finding out we were headed to Yakima, a neighbor stopped by to tell me about Gasperetti's.

"You've got to go there," he insisted. "And don't forget to order the onion rings. They're not on the menu."

That's one piece of advice I have never forgotten. Just a few weeks ago, my wife, Leslie, and I feasted on yet another basket of hand-cut, sweet onion rings. The quarter-inch-thick rings tasted as good as they did three decades ago. Mario would have been proud of his son.

Now that's worth boasting about, even if it is top secret.

# Wine judging gets the juices flowing

*June 18, 2006*

Being a wine judge has little to do with sipping and everything to do with spitting. And I'm not talking about a few spits and spats. We're talking several gallons worth.

The very thought of spitting out any kind of wine, whether it's good, bad or smelling of diesel fuel, is something foreign to me. During my formative years of wine tasting — we're talking college here — judging a quality wine amounted to passing around a bottle of slightly chilled Mateus Rose, splashing the thin reddish liquid into a Mason jar and exclaiming with an emphatic smack of the lips: "I feel the headache already starting." Back then, the worse the headache, the better the wine.

But my Neanderthal approach to wine took a U-turn several weeks ago when Ruth Anglin, activities manager at the Central Washington State Fair, invited me to be a guest wine judge. Not familiar with my Mateus-Rose upbringing, she actually thought it would be a grand idea for me to join a panel of wine experts at one of the state's oldest competitive events: the Washington State Wine Competition.

Under Anglin's gentle and expert guidance over the past 25 years, the competition has become one of the premier judging events in the state. For this year's contest, 78 wineries entered 337 wine varieties — from cabernet sauvignon to pinot gris and sauvignon blanc.

What's left over after the judges leave — a sea of wine bottles.

Before Anglin had asked me to try my hand — or rather tongue — at wine judging, I never thought much about what it takes to declare a sangiovese a gold-medal winner or another one roadkill because it leaves behind an aroma of iodine. Wine judging, though, is serious business these days, especially with this state's wine industry trying to rub shoulders with California's famed valleys of Napa and Sonoma. It's also hard work, as I found out when I entered the Modern Living Building at State Fair Park for a day's worth of wine sipping.

First, it started at the ungodly hour of 8 a.m. How could anyone, let alone a neophyte wine taster like myself, possibly decipher the fruity splash of a syrah when your taste buds are still throbbing from last night's supersized helping of spicy Thai food?

Have no fear, Anglin and her team of volunteers knew how to handle this. You start off the day with — what else? — a practice sip. That's right, it's like whacking a bucket of golf balls. Tiger Woods wouldn't dare head off to the first hole at the Masters without banging out several hundred golf balls from the practice tee.

So it goes for wine judges.

For our practice gulp, we were served a chilled white wine. I later found out it wasn't even a U.S. wine, but an Aussie import — a Yellow Tail chardonnay. Despite being a "jug" wine, it seemed to have done the trick. Everyone swilled, spat and smiled.

Now with our palates cleansed and our noses filled with tantalizing aromas of vanilla and fresh fruit, our panel of five judges (six if you toss in me) went about our business — tasting 130 wines. Don't think for a minute we lounged around enjoying such delights as the soft, unfolding rewards of a $50-a-bottle cabernet. It was sniff, slurp and spit — with the emphasis on spit.

And where do these slurps end up? In a square plastic container that looked remarkably like the white ice-cube containers you find in not-so-ritzy motel rooms. How elegant. None of this seemed to faze our panel. I also learned, contrary to conventional wisdom, wine judges are not snobs. Far from it. No black ties or tuxedo cummerbunds here. A few wore shorts and sandals. T-shirts seemed OK.

And no, they didn't talk shop and babble on about wines all day. Instead, conversations often tended toward the plight of the Mariners and which Monty Python movie is the funniest ("The Holy Grail" got my vote).

Andy Perdue, an accomplished wine judge and writer, led our panel. He served as the arbiter of refined tastes, meaning he engaged the other judges in speaking up for or against the wines they were spitting out.

Though he liked to extol the virtues of Washington wines he tasted, Perdue didn't hesitate to lower the boom when flaws showed up in a wine, whether it was due to a lousy cork or fumbled winemaking. The other judges also were up to the task.

One of their favorite ways of describing a flawed wine, besides saying it reminded them of dirty socks, was noting it had the lingering stench of a dripping wet dog. In one tasting, a petite syrah came off so poorly that the judges tripped over themselves in finding the best smelly-dog description. Finally, Perdue summed up the awful taste: It's like Lassie saving Timmy downstream from a pulp mill.

Well, you get the idea.

Rarely did this panel of pros disagree. It was uncanny. After a flight of wines was tasted, each judge would go up to a flip chart and jot down their votes: "e" for eliminate and "r" for retain. Three votes were necessary to retain or eliminate a wine. The same held true for gold, silver and bronze medals.

As I said, they tended to agree on the wines, except for one judge. Me. I was off the chart, literally. The worst happened with No. 119. A merlot.

I sniffed, slurped and noted on my pad of paper: "good taste." I had given up trying to wow the judges with the overwrought adjectives that are so popular with wine writers. I couldn't tell boysenberry from candied orange — and forget about finding anything remotely smelling of tar or tobacco. Try as hard as I could, when I sniffed a wine and later took a mouthful, the best I could come up with was "nice smell" or, as in this case, "good taste."

Anyway, I was fairly confident I had this one right. Then came the voting. Each judge put down an "e." No hesitation.

"Gee, I thought it was good," I said. Heads turned in my direction.

The guest judge had spoken. Suddenly the aroma of a dripping wet dog filled the room.

# Eat your way to happiness

*October 5, 2008*

The death-spiral of the stock market these past few weeks has done wonders for the makers of Tums. Acid indigestion is now a part of the American dream.

That's especially true for those of us who foolishly keep checking the status of our retirement funds. Talk about your stomach doing back-flips. Mine did a two-and-a-half-gainer on Monday. I confess a singlewide trailer is looking more appealing all the time.

This high anxiety, of course, builds up stress. This is not good for our bodies. Blood pressure shoots up. Bags begin to form like snowdrifts under the eyes. It's not a pretty sight.

So what are we to do? Are we to give up and let today's economic apocalypse bury us in house foreclosures, bad credit ratings and junk bonds?

Not a chance. My advice: Eat your way to health. Grab a foot-long corn dog — a pig on a stick — and take a bite out of heaven.

It's all about comfort food.

I don't care if it means slurping down a bowl of hot chicken soup or inhaling a quart of Ben & Jerry's chocolate chip cookie dough ice cream. If it makes you smile, go ahead and stuff your gullet. This is the kind of medicine we need right now, packed with hundreds, perhaps thousands of needless calories that we know we'll never burn off. Who cares? Our battle cry is "carpe diem" — live for the moment.

But for only today. In a short few hours, gates to the Central Washington State Fair will close and gone will be the sweet smell of barbecued chicken and freshly baked cinnamon rolls.

The fair is our holy grail of comfort food. It's the mecca for munchies, for all things battered and fried. The choices are breath-taking and heart-stopping: fried onion rings, fried egg rolls, beer-battered fries, fried cheesecake, fried oyster sandwich and crispitos, a concoction of chicken and jalapeno peppers wrapped up in a tortilla and then fried.

As you can see, the key process here is frying everything that's edible in hot oil, and then watching the oil ooze out as you cradle the hot morsels in a pristine white napkin. Poetry in motion.

Researchers who study monkeys for a living have long proven that comfort food eases stress. It literally calms the savage beasts. Instead of serving Ben & Jerry's, the animal researchers dish out banana-flavored pellets. Produce more stress; deliver more pellets. If the proper amount of comfort food is given, the monkeys will chortle in unison.

The same is true for us humans. It happened last Sunday when my wife and I introduced my cousin and his wife, who recently moved to Ellensburg, to the wonders of our state fair. After discussing the sad state of both our nation's economy and our savings accounts, we went directly to the food booths. In the span of two short hours, we consumed four roast beef sandwiches, a bratwurst buried in grilled onions, three corn dogs, a fried Twinkie and a stack of fried Oreos.

And guess what? We left the fairgrounds still hungry. That's the power of comfort food. The more calories you choke down, the more you crave.

So let's see how many calories we can actually rack up grazing through the food booths at the fair.

Let's begin with a nice appetizer. How about a plate of curly fries? Calories: 620.

Now let's try a Young Life roast beef sandwich. This is a fair standard. You can't go home without one. Calories: 610.

Don't forget the foot-long corn dog. That's a must. Calories: 375.

Let's kick it up a notch. The Harrah Christian School's "Ultimate" Burger is in a class by itself. The Ultimate is a one-half pound beef patty on a bun the size of a large Frisbee, topped with four ounces of ham, cheese, lettuce, tomatoes and onions. Did I mention Tums before? Calories: 1,090.

Care for something international? The fair has Greek food, so let's nibble on a gyro with its spiced meat and yogurt. Calories: 680.

Want something from South of the Border? Let's traipse over to the Mexican Grill, the newest addition to the fair's food vendors, and order up a soft corn taco with chicken. Calories: 210.

Now it's on to the fried onions. The choices are endless. How about the food booth that's near the Budweiser Stage. Here, more than 50 pounds of Colossus onions are sliced and fried up each day. Calories for a full onion: 1,300.

Of course, we can't forget the desserts. My first treat ever at the fair was a funnel cake, showered in powdered sugar. Calories: 760.

What's a fair without elephant ears? These deep-fried pastries have become a cult favorite. Calories: 310.

And then there's the Selah Heights Grange's Dairy Bar, located near the horse and cow barns where the aromas can be a bit intimidating. A large vanilla and chocolate swirl ice cream cone does the trick. Calories: 930.

For this perfectly delicious day of comfort-food consumption, my calculator reads 6,885 calories. That's about four days' worth of caloric intake for an adult. This would immediately qualify you for TV's "Biggest Loser" and a visit to Yakima Valley Memorial Hospital's emergency room.

Though comfort food is what we need and crave, please note that by treading water for 10 straight hours at a medium pace, all of these 6,885 calories can be burned off, allowing you to start over again with a clean slate.

With the way our economy is headed, treading water may be the best we can hope for.

# Confessions of a wine klutz

It's always red wine that's spilled, perhaps a malbec or a spicy syrah. It's never something white like Treveri's sparkling Blanc de Blanc, which requires a light dab from a napkin and it's forgotten.

But red wine is another matter entirely. It ruins clothes, carpets, even friendships if you happen to chuck French Bordeaux across a priceless tablecloth that's been in your host's family for three generations. Yes, I've done that, and much more.

I once swept my hand across a dinner table when making a joke and toppled over not one but three wine glasses brimming with freshly poured L'Ecole No. 41 merlot. It's one of those immutable laws of nature whenever a dinner party is held or friends gather for lively conversation — wine will be spilled.

And it never happens in secret, in the dark. Instead, the spotlight is on you as everyone gasps in horror as you send a gusher of wine heavenward. You try to smile through the catcalls and jeers but it's no good, the stain on your ever-diminishing sense of dignity is as irremovable as that blood-red puddle soaking ever so quickly into the ivory white carpet beneath your feet.

Worse yet, there comes a time when you dunk yourself in a full glass of wine. Hasn't happened to you yet? It will, trust me. My moment came at a wine tasting event years ago set up by the Yakima Kiwanis Club, of which I'm a longtime member.

I arrived a bit late and sat down at a table packed with attentive Kiwanis members, their glasses filled with a well-aged cabernet as they swirled and sniffed the complex aromas rising up from the goblet. After filling my glass, I too began to swirl the silky wine and looked up at Wade Wolfe, renowned winemaker of Thurston Wolfe winery in Prosser, discussing what flavors we would soon be enjoying.

Excited about actually taking my first sip, I raised the wine glass to my lips, a ritual that heretofore had come quite natural to me. Not that night. Somehow the glass slipped from my hand. It fell like a rock toward the table. I instinctively clutched at the stem in hopes of keeping the wine glass from toppling over. That rather violent act caused an unexpected chain reaction — like Yellowstone's Old Faithful geyser, the wine shot straight up into the air. Whoosh. The cabernet splashed my face. Red droplets sluiced down my cheeks, with one rather large drop clinging desperately to the bony end of my nose.

Stunned by what had happened, I looked around for what I imagined would be a thunderclap of laughter. Nothing. Everyone was so intent on listening to the gifted winemaker that my gaffe appeared to go unnoticed. I grabbed several napkins off the table and quickly mopped up my face. I dodged a bullet this time, I chuckled to myself.

"Did I really see that happen," came a voice to my right. A fellow Kiwanian tried her best to keep from busting a gut. She poured me another glass of wine and smiled. "Try to hit your mouth this time, OK?"

Besides wine tastings, another potential minefield for spillages is a high school class reunion. Didn't see that coming, did you? Well, neither did I until I went to a gathering at the Yakima Valley Museum for the Eisenhower High School class of 1970. A graduate of that class, my wife Leslie convinced me it would be fun and even bought me a colorful blue Ralph Lauren polo shirt for the occasion. This time I decided to go with white wine to lessen the chances of doing damage to others and myself.

Little did I know one of Leslie's classmates would serve as the klutz this time. He greeted me as if I were a fellow classmate, figuring my white hair and mustache were a disguise on my part. Sorry, I said, I went to school in the Chicago area. That remark prompted him to make an offhand joke about my hapless Chicago Cubs never winning a World Series in a century. Just then he got something caught in his throat. He coughed, his body shaking wildly along with the hand that held his wine glass. A ball of ruby red wine gushed forth and scored a direct hit on the front of my new shirt.

Panic ensued. Leslie sent me immediately off to the restroom to soak the stain in cold water. For the rest of the evening I walked around in my Ralph Lauren logo shirt dripping with water. I'm sure Leslie's classmates thought I had contracted some rare, and contagious, perspiration disorder for no one during the rest of the evening approached me to ask whether I was a former Ike grad. In a way, I appreciated the solitude.

So my advice to those of you who raise a glass of red wine in celebration of life, think twice about that gesture. If spilled, it comes with a price — your self-esteem.

# The joys and jitters of eating raw food

*March 6, 2015*

**E**ating exotic food means giving your taste buds the ultimate experience. And that requires one thing — eating it raw. No grilling, sautéing or roasting allowed. It has to be excitingly fresh, without pretense or guile.

That's what I did back in 2002 when I sat down at a table at Joe Allen's restaurant in the heart of the theater district in New York City, just a block from Times Square. I was with a group of reporters from the Yakima Herald-Republic, where I worked back then as city editor. We were in The Big Apple to receive a prestigious national award and found ourselves one night searching for a place to eat. We asked one of the contest judges to suggest a restaurant and he led us to Joe Allen's.

The cozy restaurant thrives on those attending Broadway shows. Back when it opened in 1965, it served up hamburgers for 75 cents and began to paper its walls in a most unusual way, with posters from Broadway flops beginning with "Kelly," which lasted just one show.

It was 8 p.m. when we arrived, a perfect time to be there since the plays on Broadway were already in full swing. We sat in the middle of the dining room, giving us a full view of the bar and a table in the corner near the kitchen. I mention this table because sitting at it were two bona fide celebrities — Al Pacino, star of the "Godfather" movies, and Beverly D'Angelo, movie actress and mother of his two children. The contest judge told us in no uncertain terms not to bother the famous couple, so we didn't. We just stared and realized how far we really were from Yakima.

That realization sunk in even deeper when I scanned the menu and came upon these two words: steak tartare. I knew what those words translated to — raw meat. And I knew I couldn't resist.

The chilled beef, often from the choicest cut of beef tenderloin, is cut into bite-sized pieces and blended with a mixture of capers, onions, pepper and Worcestershire. Often it's topped with a fresh egg yolk as it was back in the 1930s in Paris when the French called the dish *steack à l'Americaine*. At Joe Allen's, I don't remember the egg adorning the beef but I do recall it being served with bite-sized toast points and arugula.

When the waiter placed the steak tartare in front of me, others at the table started to make fake gagging sounds to see if I would turn pea-green. I didn't flinch but I could distinctly see Pacino scowling at our antics, reminiscent of his character Michael Corleone when he ordered yet another Mafia boss to be whacked.

Undeterred by Pacino and my fellow journalists, I bit down on the bright red meat. I didn't gag, but the taste sensation was quite unlike anything I had ever experienced before. I could definitely taste the capers. The cold feel of the meat lingered as I forced myself to swallow. I quickly took a big gulp of wine. It's surprising how a well-crafted pinot noir can save the day.

However, no amount of wine could have bailed me out last fall when my wife Leslie and I sat down for dinner at Cambio de Tercio, a delightful Spanish tapas restaurant in London's Kensington district. It was a Friday night, the final day of our two-week visit to England. The small narrow restaurant was packed with patrons, their voices mingling with the dulcet sounds from a guitarist strumming a 12-string guitar.

Our waiter, a native of Spain, couldn't have been nicer. He pointed out some of the restaurant's unusual tapas — cuttlefish meatballs cooked in ink and ox tail caramelized in red wine. What really attracted my eye was an entrée featuring razor clams.

"We have those in the Pacific Northwest," I told the waiter. "I love them."

My mind flashed to a vision of fried razor clam strips piled up alongside an equally enormous stack of french fries. But like most things in life, what you expect is not what you get.

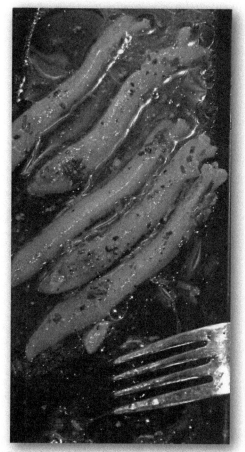

Razor clams, from Spain not the Pacific Northwest.

When the waiter arrived with my order, I asked breathlessly, "Are these my razor clams?"

I had hoped they weren't. Before me, in a small oblong dish, lay five wormlike creatures resting in a sauce of lime juice, sherry and heaven knows what else.

The waiter was undeterred by my question and replied with a smile, "Now watch this."

He then reached over and plucked out a toothpick from a small container on our table. He raised the toothpick above one of the thin, tubular clams and poked at it.

Guess what? It moved. The damn thing was alive.

I gasped loudly and Leslie let out a well-measured but distinctly audible scream. With patrons in the restaurant now riveted on my next move, I had little choice. As the saying goes, "When in Rome do as the Romans do," so I grabbed my fork and speared one of the clams. With the bivalve writhing on the tines of my fork, I munched down on the fresh razor clam. Its rubbery texture was not revolting, but not appealing either.

When I asked Leslie if she wanted a taste, she looked at me coldly and offered this curt reply: "I don't think so."

That works for me. I can stomach raw beef perhaps. But when it comes to a $30 entrée trying to wriggle out of my mouth, all bets are off. I mean really, do you want a worm doing somersaults in your stomach? I don't think so.

# A dinner disaster with a purr-fect ending

*November 7, 2014*

Mention the words "dinner party" and the first thing that comes to my mind isn't the image of master chef Wolfgang Puck serving his signature dish of angel hair pasta with goat cheese and thyme, but rather that of the Titanic taking a nosedive underneath the polar ice cap.

Dinner disasters come in all shapes and sizes, and often have nothing to do with the selected menu, ingredients or prep work. Instead, these kitchen catastrophes may have everything to do with four-legged pets that inhabit our homes. They may be cute and fun to play with, but never forget they are always finding ways to satisfy that one primordial urge — eating. And that means feasting on something other than dry chunks of Purina Dog Chow or Science Diet for fat cats.

I learned this lesson the hard way one warm summer's day when my late wife, Bronnie, and I invited a dozen or so friends for a dinner party at our rented farmhouse near the small town of Bow, not far from Mount Vernon where I worked at the newspaper. The meal featured fresh corn, salad and bread from a local bakery and the *pièce de résistance* — a beautifully filleted steelhead that Bronnie had caught on the famed Skagit River.

By the time guests had arrived and started a spirited game of badminton in the back yard, I had already fashioned from aluminum foil a large cooking tray for the sea-run rainbow trout. I covered the steelhead in a special barbecue sauce I had found in a fishing book written by Stan Jones, a renowned Washington state angler. The sauce featured butter, tomato paste, chili powder, Worcestershire sauce, white wine vinegar and a splash of Tabasco. This marinade had a kick, plus a fragrant aroma.

Enter from stage left our cat, Shrdlu. Yes, it's an odd name for a feline unless you had worked at a newspaper and were familiar with a Linotype machine. Those six letters, shrdlu, were famous during the heyday of "hot lead" publishing since they represented some of the most common letters used by typesetters.

I spooned on the reddish sauce over the thick flanks of the steelhead and stepped outside to check on the charcoal grill. That was a fateful move. Ever the curious cat, Shrdlu decided to check out what was producing so many mouth-watering aromas. Much to my horror, I returned to the kitchen to find Shrdlu on the kitchen counter, crouched next to the edge of the aluminum tray, his thick tongue sticking out as he lapped up the sauce.

"Stop," I yelled.

Sadly that didn't prompt the desired result — scaring the cat back down onto the floor. Instead, Shrdlu did the unthinkable. He barfed all over the steelhead. And for the record books, let's just say it was no small upchuck. Most of our dinner entree was covered by Shrdlu's gastric geyser.

Bronnie heard the commotion and returned to the kitchen. Together we surveyed the wreckage. It was an oh-my-gawd moment. Now your first instinct would be to toss the fish into the garbage and call on Colonel Sanders for a bucket of fried chicken. But I couldn't imagine getting rid of that once tantalizing steelhead.

Enter Julia Child, one of America's most famous cooks. A lovable character who wouldn't think twice about flattening a plump whole chicken with a heavy mallet, Child once coined this sage advice: "Remember, if you're alone in the kitchen, who is going to see you?"

Bronnie and I both looked around and realized no one else had witnessed Shrdlu's spew. Seizing the moment, I grabbed the steelhead fillet and headed to the sink. Cold water gushed forth from the faucet and, a minute later, the fillet was as good as new. While I didn't quite get to the sink within the "five-second rule," it was close enough.

I tossed together a new batch of the sauce and headed to the grill, ready to sizzle the steelhead as if nothing had ever happened.

So was it a success? Let's just say several guests called it the best steelhead they had ever eaten. I even broke down and gave Shrdlu a sample. The cat smacked his lips with great satisfaction and purred loudly. I swore, just then, I heard the voice of Julia Child whispering, *"Bon appetite."*

# Memories

---

*"While experiencing happiness, we have difficulty in
being conscious of it. Only when the happiness is past and
we look back on it do we suddenly realize — sometimes
with astonishment — how happy we had been."*
— NIKOS KAZANTZAKIS, FROM "ZORBA THE GREEK"

# Returning home for a sentimental journey

*January 19, 2003*

L ife looks a lot different when viewed from inside a "303" cab heading out of Chicago's O'Hare Airport.

My 22-year-old son and I were on our way to Northbrook for Christmas, to the place where I grew up. Years ago, Northbrook was quaint, with one main street, a drugstore with a soda fountain stand, and a rustic tavern, the Cypress Inn, where Benny Goodman tunes held sway. Now it's an upscale northern suburb of Chicago with roomy mansions dotting the tree-lined streets.

It's a brisk 20-minute ride from the world's busiest air terminal. Though the cab ride followed the shortest route to my mother's home, it made meandering zigzags through the mind fields of my childhood.

As we entered the Northbrook town limits, I gestured out the window to a series of large brick buildings. That's where I went to high school, I told my son. He seemed unimpressed.

With the scenery whizzing by, I wondered if the school still had my name enshrined in its trophy case. As a mere freshman, I got named most valuable player on our tennis team. But it was an honor with little distinction, and no fanfare. I didn't even get a chance to accept the award at the annual spring assembly. It was canceled. Our team was miserable back then, compiling a dismal record of two wins and 14 losses. Little wonder there was no assembly. The coach was so embarrassed by the team's showing he handed me my plastic trophy in the school parking lot.

So much for getting on the cover of my high school yearbook.

Then we passed by a row of houses next to the school. That's when a memory cell suddenly popped to life. I had almost forgotten about the day a jet fell from the sky.

It happened in my senior year, in the fall of 1966. A military jet flying out of Glenview Naval Air Station went out of control. The pilot ejected and the plane veered in the direction of our high school.

The pilotless plane missed our school and slammed into a two-story wood-framed house a half-block away. I was in the cafeteria at the time and ran with scores of other students to the site of the crash.

We figured no one could have survived this explosion of metal and jet fuel, but luckily we were wrong. The lady who lived there had gone downstairs to her basement moments before the crash. She survived, as did the pilot.

By now, my son was getting interested in my past.

Next our cab drew near an intersection directly across from the First Presbyterian Church. That's the corner where Bruce Jarchow and I once were school crossing guards. Now my son really got interested, for he knew about Bruce. Everyone knew about him in Northbrook. He had gone on to fame as an actor of stage and Hollywood movies and television cameos on "Seinfeld" and "Coach." He got his start while working alongside the late John Belushi in the heydays of Chicago's famed Second City comedy club. Back in elementary school Bruce and I were close friends. We would lock arms as we merrily danced our way from Meadowbrook Elementary School to the street corner across from the church. Ah, fond memories of being important when it really mattered.

A few days into our trip, I jogged through town, a ritual I try to do each time I visit my mom's home. My running took me over the north branch of the Chicago River, where the town got its name, to the same school crossing where Bruce and I were once stationed 40 years ago. It's now guarded by a stoplight.

There was little traffic at the corner that morning except for a single car. It was heading toward me, but had its left-turn signal on. So I sprinted ahead. I heard the squeal of tires and saw the car a few feet away, steam surging from its radiator. The driver had decided not to turn after all. I leapt out of the way, and stopped. My heart was pounding. Now that would have been something,

I thought to myself. Getting punched out at the very corner where I once stood as a crossing guard. What irony.

Maybe returning to your childhood memories isn't a safe trip after all.

But you can't escape them. I found that out again on Christmas Eve when my family went to the 11 p.m. service at the First Presbyterian Church. When we entered, we were each handed a candle. Later in the service, the overhead lights were turned off, and we were plunged into darkness except for a single candle held by the minister. Walking down from the altar to the parishioners below, the minister took that candle and tipped it to one side, igniting the wick of another. And so the process continued, the flame being passed along from candle to candle, until everyone sitting in the church was touched by a halo of honey-dewed light.

It's funny how childhood memories flicker, like so many candles, lighting our lives where darkness too often intrudes.

In the glow of my candle, I peered down the long aisle of the church and recalled when I was a boy, only 8 or 9 years old, scurrying toward the front of the church, the pews filled with a congregation of adults, among them my mom and dad. It was the morning of my confirmation into the church, a solemn occasion. My passage, though, was anything but quiet. For some reason, I had stuck a small bell in my pocket. Each time I took a step, the bell would resonate, filling the church with what I imagined was laughter.

When I reached the Rev. Harry Lundell, he handed me my Bible and grimaced. I thought I heard him say, "You never go quietly, do you?"

I then clanged my way outside to the bright sunlight, a stone's throw away from the corner where I once stood guard.

# Teachers find a way to make an impact

*May 21, 2001*

N o two teachers are alike.
That universal truth became strikingly clear when I scanned the faces gazing back at me during the recent Crystal Apple Awards ceremony. Among the more than 250 people crammed into the conference room were 15 very gifted educators, all from the Yakima School District, who were being honored for their extraordinary work with students.

I had a difficult assignment that afternoon. I was there to regale those 15 exceptional school leaders, and their families and friends and countless supporters, with stories about the teachers who had made a difference in my life.

Not an easy assignment, especially when I had to conjure up images of myself as a young student. It's not a pretty self-portrait: big buck teeth caged in silver braces, thick glasses smeared with thumbprints and a mouth that never stopped chattering, a condition that once forced my first-grade teacher to tape my mouth shut. Yes, wondrous images of a boy yearning to be anyone other than himself.

Needless to say, more than one exceptional teacher would be needed to fix this fine mess. So I decided to talk about two of my favorite teachers.

One of them was a teacher I had at Glenbrook North High School in Northbrook, Illinois, the northern suburb of Chicago where I grew up.

He taught one of the most obscure subjects you could imagine. It's no longer part of any high school curriculum, and that's a pity. The subject is

Latin, the language of Julius Caesar and ancient Rome, the very foundation of the English language. I chose Latin based solely on my older brother's recommendation.

"It's a duck," my brother opined, referring to the ease of getting an "A" in the class. "You don't even have to speak it."

That's all I needed to hear. What I didn't bargain on was the teacher. He turned out to be one of the most eccentric teachers I would ever know. Maybe that's why I took the course for four straight years.

His name was Mr. Van Dyke.

Now we had some teachers at our high school that looked like they walked straight out of Gentleman's Quarterly. I had a history teacher who had the Hollywood flair — blond hair, blue eyes and a permanent tan. When he walked down the hallways, girls would swoon.

Not so with Mr. Van Dyke. When he walked down those same hallways, the girls would shriek in terror.

To put it bluntly, Mr. Van Dyke was oddly shaped, like a large, over-ripened pear. His oval face was topped with black, thinning hair that roamed riotously over his pointed head. He wore thick, black-rimmed glasses that only helped accentuate his bulging eyes, which seemed ready to burst. His shirt refused to be tucked in, and his tie, always black and pencil-thin, hung crazily from his neck. Call him "disheveled" and you would be paying him a compliment.

But what a wonderful teacher he was. He never went by the book. Never.

Sure we learned to recite Caesar's famous expression: "Veni, Vidi, Vinci" (I came, I saw, I conquered). But Mr. Van Dyke's brain was too stuffed with ideas to keep us merely translating Caesar's Gallic Wars. No, we dabbled in the lurid lyrics of Catullus, a rather controversial writer who was the Henry Miller of his day. We also discussed Hegel the philosopher and Dylan Thomas the great Irish poet.

Mr. Van Dyke loved plays and modern playwrights, and so we would create impromptu theater productions in class. Once we wrote a play in the style of Tennessee Williams, putting Stanley Kowalski of "A Streetcar Named Desire" in an imaginary debate with Cicero, Rome's most famous orator.

It was bad theater, but that didn't bother Mr. Van Dyke. He howled with glee. But we didn't stop there. For class discussions, Mr. Van Dyke talked of death and of suicide, of murder and of war, of Kennedy's Peace Corps and of LBJ's Vietnam, of teens having sex too soon and teens not having sex at all.

Back in the mid-1960s, those weren't topics you heard bandied about in high school, let alone in a class where the language being studied had ceased to exist centuries earlier.

That's what Mr. Van Dyke did. He made you think beyond yourself. He exploded your mind with ideas, and left you searching for more.

And then there are teachers of the heart.

I had a very special one in Miss Durcany. She was my fourth-grade teacher. All of us adored her. She was a tall, statuesque woman, with a round face and a smile that melted you on the spot. In class, we eagerly sought her attention, waiting to hear her sweetly say, "Very nice lettering. Those are the best 'w's' I've ever seen." But what really set Miss Durcany apart from my other teachers was what she did outside of the classroom.

She was a dance teacher. All the fourth-graders from our elementary school were enrolled. That was the thing to do back then.

Though most of us were painfully inept on the dance floor, Miss Durcany never gave up hope. She taught us the fox trot, a little cha-cha-cha and the hat dance. Most of all, we learned how to waltz. And each night, one song would be reserved for the teacher. Before anyone was allowed to dance, Miss Durcany would go out into the gym and select a partner.

Guess who got picked? Me. And there we would be, just the two of us, dancing the waltz, in front of everyone.

What a great rush for a fourth-grader.

I made a point of never stepping on her toes. I always thanked her for the dance, made a short, awkward bow and returned to my chair, to a chorus of catcalls laced with "teacher's pet." I didn't mind that in the least. In fact, that's exactly what I wanted to be.

Great teachers never leave your life. And so it was with Miss Durcany.

Some 30 years later, I returned to my hometown again, to attend the funeral for my brother who had died of a heart attack at the age of 45. After the memorial service was over, our family greeted the hundreds of people who had attended.

I didn't see her at first, but I heard the voice.

"Remember me?"

I didn't have to look up this time as I did in fourth grade, but looked straight ahead. And there she was: Miss Durcany, my dance partner for life. We hugged and shared tears, and a few good laughs.

And yes, she still remembered the waltz. She said she had never forgotten. Great teachers never do.

# Taking a swing at baseball and the God particle

*"... one of the conditions of enlightenment has always been a willingness to let go of what we thought we knew in order to appreciate truths we had never dreamed of."*
— KAREN ARMSTRONG, THEOLOGIAN

*April 4, 2013*

With the major league baseball season in full swing and the hope of a trip to the World Series still possible, it's timely to ask: What does a Higgs boson subatomic particle have to do with the Seattle Mariners' Edgar Martinez?

Everything.

Last month scientists in Geneva, Switzerland, announced that after analyzing data from particle collisions at the Large Hadron Collider, they had found what's referred to as the "God particle." It turns out these brainiacs in white lab coats had discovered how particles gain mass, which may help to explain the universe. It also doesn't hurt if you can conduct 1,000 billion collisions to test your theory.

Edgar Martinez, on the other hand, had to produce only one collision to create an event of equally Biblical proportions. For Mariner fans, it's simply called "The Double." It came at the bottom half of the 11th inning with the Mariners trailing by one run in the final game of the 1995 American League Division Series against the New York Yankees, a team of immense talent and a storied baseball tradition.

With Joey Cora on third base and Ken Griffey Jr. on first, Martinez belted a line drive to the base of the wall in left field. Cora scored easily and then Griffey rounded third, heading home with the winning run. He narrowly beat the throw and slid safely into home plate. The capacity crowd inside the cavernous Kingdome went wild.

It's regarded as the Mariner's biggest hit in franchise history. The Double preserved professional baseball in Seattle and gave us the miraculous spectacle of players piling on Griffey at home plate as the young slugger screamed with joy.

Of such is the game of baseball with its human drama of fleeting success and agonizing failure, where the resounding crack of a bat and ball can mimic, at exquisite moments like Martinez's game-winning hit, the Godlike qualities of Higgs boson.

"The miraculous is the grist of myth; and myth permeates religion," writes John Sexton in his recently published book, "Baseball as a Road to God: Seeing Beyond the Game."

Besides serving as president of New York University, Sexton is also a member of the faculty and teaches a class on baseball and religion where he attempts to reveal what he calls "the basic building blocks of a spiritual or religious life."

While some may find the secular world of baseball at odds with religion, I don't. I never have. And believe me, I know all about praying for wins. I grew up in the Chicago area and rooted for the hapless Cubs, a team that has not won a World Series title since 1908.

Imagine as a 9-year-old the sense of wonder I felt when first stepping into Wrigley Field in 1958 and soaking in the beauty of its manicured infield grass and the ivy-shrouded fence stretching across the outfield.

Then came the smoke, so thick it made my eyes water. Yes, back then before laws were enacted against smoking in public, old men in white short-sleeve shirts would puff away on their Roi-Tan cigars. That was my baptism.

Next came the call to worship from the vendors: "Cold beer, get your cold beer here." Baseball even affords a time for singing hymns. It's called the seventh-inning stretch when fans join together in a rousing rendition of "Take Me Out To The Ball Game."

My brother Jay outside Wrigley Field in Chicago.

Baseball also requires us to live slow and take notice of life around us, Sexton argues. No wonder baseball players round the bases in a counter-clockwise fashion. Time ceases to move and we find ourselves, as cultural historian Thomas Berry once wrote, "invaded by the world of the sacred."

That sacred moment for me took place on another visit to Wrigley Field. It was June 9, 1965. It was my older brother's 18th birthday, and my sister and I were treating him to a Cubs game. I made a bold promise: To get my big brother, Jay, a game ball that day. I arrived with my baseball glove and we found seats along the third-base line, a perfect spot for foul balls to land.

Sure enough, during batting practice before the game, the Milwaukee Braves' pitcher, Wade Blasingame, sliced a foul ball into the seats below us. I leapt to my feet and darted down the cement stairway.

However, when I reached the row of seats where the ball had landed, I was not alone. A swarm of kids had already gathered and the battle was on. We formed a small scrum, with heads down and our hands grabbing at the elusive baseball. With my right arm scratched and bleeding, I snared the ball and raised it high in the air. "I've got it," I proclaimed.

I handed the ball to my brother.

The game featured four future Hall of Fame icons — Hank Aaron and Eddie Mathews for the Braves and Ernie Banks and Billy Williams for the Cubs. In the bottom of the sixth inning with two outs and two on base, Banks deposited a home run in the left-field bleachers, giving the Cubs a 3 to 1 lead.

Next up to the plate came Cubs' catcher, Chris Krug, who promptly swatted a foul ball in our direction. There's no way I'm going after that one, I told myself. The ball hit a metal railing in the lower box seats and then another railing and another. The ball was miraculously ascending toward us.

For some reason, my brother stood up. He cupped his hands together, much like Giants' outfielder Willie Mays had done when he made his historic catch of a fly ball hit deep to center field in the opening game of the 1954 World Series at the Polo Fields in New York. The foul ball landed squarely in my brother's hands and the fans around us roared with delight.

We had gone to the game for one baseball and returned home with two.

My brother and I would attend several more Cubs games over the years. On his 45th birthday, after playing a game of tennis, he stopped to rest in a lawn chair and suffered a heart attack. He died before I could wish him a happy birthday, before we could talk one more time about the Cubs.

For my brother and me, baseball had always been our common bond, our road to God. Though it's lonely without him, I'm still on that pathway. I guess I always will be.

# Camp Dudley, where memories last a lifetime

*August 16, 1998*

*C*hildren with special needs rarely get a chance to enjoy the everyday pleasures *of simply being a kid. This is especially true when it comes to attending a summer camp. But that didn't stop me from spending four days at a YMCA camp with my son Jed, who was diagnosed with autism at age 3. Though he had limited language and social skills, he had an engaging smile and a loving personality. Four years after this column was published, Jed died following complications from a severe seizure.*

*Here's what we experienced.*

Summer camp plays tricks on you.

You try your best to prepare for it. Sleeping bags are rolled tight. You've amassed enough "Off!" bug repellent to lather up the combined student bodies of Eisenhower and Davis high schools.

Nothing, though, could have prepared my 14-year-old son, Jed, and me for the greeting we got last month when we arrived at Camp Dudley, the Yakima Family YMCA's residence camp near White Pass. Just as I was struggling to unload our canvas luggage bag stuffed to overflowing with T-shirts, socks and assorted underwear, what to my wondering eyes should appear but three eager helpers — let's call them elves — merrily singing "Ho! Ho! Ho! Merry Christmas!"

As we made our way up the steep incline to Cabin No. 8, we were treated to more surprises. Tinsel hung with care along the windows of other cabins. What's going on here, I wondered to myself as sweat began to form large droplets along my forehead.

Why worry, the elves replied. It's Christmas in July.

I should have known my return to summer camp at the overly ripe age of 49 would lead to unexpected consequences, but hearing "Jingle Bells" ricochet through the Douglas firs was almost too much to take.

There was no turning back. As a volunteer on the YMCA's camp committee for the past decade, I had spent far too much time thumbing through budget figures and not enough with the real reason Camp Dudley exists: the boys and girls at camp. It was high time I found out if Camp Dudley was delivering on its promise to provide "the experience that lasts a lifetime." And perhaps I would be lucky enough to rediscover what it's really like bunking down with teens whose closest encounter with a shower is a bar of soap wedged deep in the bottom of their duffel bags.

## Summer camps from long, long ago

It's not as if had never been to summer camp before. Growing up in the Chicago area, I spent three consecutive summers far from home. During the 1950s and '60s, Midwest parents had a decidedly different view of summer camp than exists here in the Pacific Northwest. Unlike Camp Dudley and other camps here, which are geared to weeklong stays, summer camps back then lasted two or three months. And parents sent their kids far, far away so there was no hope of a late-night hitchhike to retrieve a favorite baseball glove.

When I was 13 years old, my parents shipped me off with my older brother to a boy's camp in the farthest reaches of northern Minnesota. It was situated on an island in the middle of nowhere. The place had a boot-camp rhythm to it and was run by a director whom I was convinced was a reincarnation of Napoleon. Canoe trips into the wilderness lasted from a week to 10 days, with two-mile portages a common attraction.

The most bizarre thing that happened involved secret initiations for campers. I went through one that ended up with a herd of us young campers being tattooed across the chest with paint and ordered to run naked — that's right, without a stitch of clothing in the bug-infested north woods — until we reached a roaring bonfire.

Indeed, that's the kind of experience that lasts a lifetime, but not one I would recommend for everyone.

Jed sits on a deck at the camp's outdoor chapel overlooking Clear Lake.

## Bon appétit, campers!

Thankfully, at Camp Dudley, there were no initiations or military boot-camp conditions. In fact, it seemed at times to be more like a cheerleading camp than anything else. The energy level rose throughout the day as counselors engaged the campers in games, water sports, archery, mountain biking, hiking and lots of singing (Christmas songs, what else?).

If anything makes or breaks a summer camp, it's the food. I forgot how much summer camp is built on such gastronomic delights as bug juice (or if you want to be polite, Kool-Aid), stacks of plate-sized pancakes, and that dreamy concoction of chocolate, graham crackers and toasted marshmallows, better known to freckled-faced 10-year-olds as s'mores.

At Camp Dudley, though, eating is not something you take for granted. The camp takes the old saw — "singing for your supper" — to new heights.

When entering the newly rebuilt Harvey Hunt Hall for a meal, it's a nonstop musical. There are songs for just about every occasion. There's a song introducing the dispersal of mail. Then there's another ditty that is sung when someone gets too much mail (six letters in a day sends you to the pool for a dunking, or to the lake if enough campers and counselors holler, "Lake! Lake! Lake!").

And heaven forbid you are late to a meal. Don't try to sneak in, as some tried. After the camper is apprehended, the public humiliation follows. But at Dudley, it's always lighthearted. In the case of being late to a meal, the miscreants have to perform what I delicately call the "backward crab walk." First, they plop their butts down on the floor, then prop themselves high in the air on their hands and feet. The object is to scramble across the floor. The "crabbers" perform their punishment before a jeering crowd of gleeful campers.

You begin to wonder how anyone gets a chance to eat a meal. They somehow do, as testified by the empty plastic plates stacked precariously high at the end of mealtime.

You cannot leave the table until you and your fellow cabin-mates sing yet another tune. My favorite was "Deck the Halls," sung by the assembled 89 campers in what sounded like 18 distinct foreign languages. It was hypnotic.

## Never a dull moment for counselors

Coming up with songs to be sung at camp largely falls on the shoulders of the counselors. Actually, most everything falls upon the counselors. Without a motivated staff, a summer camp comes to a grinding and inglorious halt. Thankfully, Camp Dudley had a cadre of great counselors.

Don't expect, though, to refer to them by their real names. Anonymity at Camp Dudley is taken, like everything else, to the extreme. When I first referred to the camp director by his real name, I got summarily chastised.

"I'm Elvis," he said. I didn't laugh, but I inexplicably had a sudden craving for jelly doughnuts.

Then there was "Biscuit." If you guessed she was the cook, you get an extra helping of barbecued ribs, the traditional end-of-the-week meal she serves to campers and their parents.

Besides Elvis, the counselors and assistants included Kiwi (an international Y counselor from Holland), Carrot (a natural name for someone with red hair), Barbie (platinum blonde? You betcha), Darkman (a favorite among campers and the counselor picked as the one most likely to be tossed into the pool), and the two counselors in our cabin, Juice (a veteran counselor and the camp's best basketball player) and Wolf (a delightful young man who recently graduated from Eisenhower and is preparing for a four-year stint in the Army).

While I do not regard myself as an expert when it comes to camp counselors, I confess I have rarely come upon such an enthusiastic bunch of dedicated young men and women. They actually liked being camp counselors. Can you imagine that? They are up at 6 a.m. and don't really take a break until lights-out at 10 p.m. They get all the campers involved in activities, attend to their bumps and bruises, and listen intently to their rambling monologues about snake sightings.

And for all of this, they get a salary far less than a corporate exec's, free rent in a bunk bed and one full night off a week.

Who are these people? I want them cloned immediately.

## Cabin No. 8: Bunking down at night

When you get down to the task of peeling away the layers of summer camp, its central core still has to be learning to get along with your cabin-mates. While sociologists like to ramble on about America's ability to blend divergent cultures, they invariably fail to mention summer camp. Forget the boroughs of New York City. Try a week in Cabin 8 at Camp Dudley.

Taking a selfie outside Cabin No. 8 in the spring of 2016.

In our 12-bunk cabin, we had a cross-section of America that would rival any demographic breakdown devised by the U.S. Census Bureau. We had white Anglo-Saxons, non-white Hispanics, sons of the affluent, sons of farmers and one old man (that's me).

An added plus about Camp Dudley — scholarship campers. These campers either qualify for a partial or full-ride scholarship that covers their $225 camp fees. Our cabin had several campers who made it to Dudley through the generosity of others.

And the mix of these diverse campers worked well in our cabin. Sure, there were the shoving matches. One camper didn't seem to get along with anyone else. But that always seems to be the case in summer camps. Every cabin tends to have an outsider, as it does a natural leader whose word holds sway with the others.

The cabin's leader turned out to be a scholarship camper. He was older than the others. He had turned 16, and made no secret that he had come from the rough side of town. He wore gang paraphernalia: the knit cap and the long, winter coat familiar to youth gangs roaming the downtown streets of Yakima, Toppenish, Wapato or Sunnyside.

In fact, he proudly boasted that his father was in prison — for the third time. When asked what nickname he went by, the 16-year-old made it clear he wasn't playing second fiddle to anyone: "My name is Zeus, god of all the gods."

Yes, we had the hurler of thunderbolts in our cabin. Still, his gruff exterior soon gave way, revealing a warm, engaging personality.

He seemed particularly attached to my son Jed and protected him as if he were his younger brother. It was an unexpected treat to see Zeus hold Jed's hand and lead him to the dinner table so they could sit together. One morning when Jed pointed to an empty platter of pancakes, Zeus jumped up and scowled at the other campers: "Well, who's going to get Jed some more pancakes?" Bedlam followed as Jed's fellow cabin-mates tried to grab the platter and be the first to head off to the serving line.

That's the wonder of summer camps. Friendships are forged between the most unlikely of campers.

Zeus also served as the philosopher king of the cabin. He offered up a never-ending stream of questions that kept our cabin buzzing with freewheeling conversations. Zeus once interrupted a meandering discussion about the virtues of the Sony Playstation over the Nintendo 64-game system by asking everyone, "Do you believe in life after death?"

That question forced several campers to wonder about the existence of God, whom everyone finally agreed did indeed exist. Then came a follow-up question from Zeus about whether there was life on another planet. One camper in an upper bunk near mine chimed in like a Carl Sagan impersonator, reasoning that with the "billions and billions" of stars in the universe, there just had to be life like ours out there waiting to be discovered.

No one, though, pondered whether that meant there were also parallel summer camps scattered throughout the universe.

While questions about the universe hung there in the shadows of the cabin, Zeus plowed ahead into another thorny topic: the theory of evolution.

"Do you think we came from monkeys?" he wondered aloud. Several campers, each talking at the same time — a ritual that is endlessly played out in summer camp cabins throughout the world — tried to balance teachings of Darwin with the story of Adam and Eve. I tried to wade in with my own contribution from the playwright George Bernard Shaw who once coined this gem: "Man is nothing more than an ape who shaves."

My quote, though, didn't gather much support. Finally, the discourse on evolution came to a resounding finale when a young camper exclaimed in a voice that was a bit too shrill, "I believe in the monkey!"

A moment of silence followed that exhortation. Then one of our counselors saved the day by asking what everyone else was thinking.

"What the hell does that mean?"

Ah, summer camp. There's no way to duplicate it.

## Suddenly it's over

During our abbreviated four days of summer camp Jed and I survived on a steady diet of pancakes bathed in thick maple syrup and bags of Cheetos, which we bought at the camp store. We hiked to the nearby Clear Lake dam and explored creek beds and bridges made of fallen logs. We rode our tandem bicycle around the lake with our cabin-mates, swam each day in the pool, decorated pine cones with glitter during arts and crafts, and sent arrows whistling past their targets.

Summer camp is filled with friendly faces and handshakes lasting forever. It is a time when boys and girls can be simply that — young, without a care in the world. It's when games like "Capture the Flag" become the most important 30 minutes of a young camper's life.

As the campers grow older and have to deal with corporate deadlines and 401(k) retirement plans, they will realize these days of summer are too few. Will Kool-Aid ever taste as sweet? Probably not. Will songs ever sound as whimsical or as raucous as those sung at campfire when the Big Dipper had twinkled so serenely overhead? Probably never.

I remember Zeus asking me another one of his rapid-fire questions. It stuck with me as my son and I drove away from Camp Dudley back home.

"Do you believe in mythology?" he asked.

I told him I didn't, not really knowing what he had meant.

I see now that I am an unwitting believer in myths. According to the ancient Greeks, Hebe was the goddess of youth. The daughter of Hera and Zeus, she served as the cupbearer to the gods. And once, Hebe granted an old charioteer a wonderful gift, to be youthful again for an entire day.

My gift from Hebe lasted a bit longer. Maybe it had something to do with singing "Jingle Bells" in July.

*FOOTNOTE: Years later, I asked a former YMCA camp director whatever happened to Zeus. He told me the one-time gang member had turned his life around. He earned a scholarship and went on to college, where he received a degree — the first in his family. I never had my doubts about Zeus. I credit his success to the Camp Dudley experience.*

# Tribute trees offer more than shade

*May 19, 2013*

On a sunny afternoon last week, I stopped by the Milky Way. I reached it after crossing a carpet of lush green grass at the Yakima Area Arboretum. I stood before its outstretched arms and read aloud its Latin name — *Cornus kousa*. It's a Chinese dogwood with the fanciful nickname of "Milky Way" and bears beneath its crown of thin branches a plaque: "In memory of Bronnie and Jed Hatton."

We planted the dogwood a year ago in tribute to my late wife and son.

Our "Milky Way" has good company. A few yards away stands "Venus," another *Kousa* dogwood. It's very showy this time of year with its large buttery-white blossoms cupped like a child's hand. It's dedicated in memory of Martin Howell, a friend of mine and my wife, Leslie. In life Martin was as singular as the tree growing in his honor.

And it had to be a dogwood. A Japanese maple or oak would never do. That's because Martin was an unrepentant dog lover. Martin could never turn his back on a dog in need, whether it was wandering the median strip along Interstate 82 or loping down the middle of Yakima Avenue.

He never forgot his four-legged friends. In his backyard, Martin planted Aspen trees in tribute to his dearly departed pets, including one of his favorites, Farnaby, a floppy-eared Springer mix dreaded by many for his ornery temperament but adored by Martin. When he died, Martin bequeathed his estate to the Humane Society of Central Washington, whose shelter on Nob Hill Boulevard is a short walk from Martin's "Venus."

So a living memorial tree — a dogwood — seemed a perfect way to remember Martin.

For me, a memorial tree seemed a perfect fit, too. It also solved a nagging problem: What to do with the ashes of my late wife and son? I had intended to spread the ashes across the blue waters of Lake Roosevelt where we had spent many summers fishing and camping.

The lake, though, is too remote. A tree, on the other hand, stands before you, a singular object taking root in the earth where spring rains can wash its leaves and a summer's breeze, borne from the slopes of the Cascade Mountains, can stir its stiff branches.

So my thoughts turned to the Yakima Area Arboretum, home to more than 120 memorial trees. I didn't have to worry about the ashes. Jheri Ketcham, one of the arboretum's co-executive directors, assured me there would be no problem burying them along with the tree.

"It's organic," she said of the ashes.

The contract is simple. For $1,000, you receive a memorial tree with a five-year guarantee. That's right. If the tree doesn't take root in the first year, the arboretum will replace it — no hassle, no fee. If it dies off the following winter, the same holds true. It often takes three years for a tree to come to fruition, so the guarantee makes sense.

That doesn't mean, though, you get to pick whatever kind of tree you want. Choices are limited to certain areas of the arboretum. Since we favored a dogwood for our living memorial, Jheri showed us a spot near Martin's "Venus." The arboretum staff dug a hole for our tree and provided shovels and extra dirt. We arrived early in the morning with a boombox so we could listen to songs that had been played at both Bronnie and Jed's memorial services. With one of Bronnie's favorite songs — Dobie Gray's "Drift Away" — filling the space among the arboretum's pine and maple trees, Leslie and I shoveled dirt around the base of our young dogwood. The setting, and the moment, felt right, like it was meant to be.

Years ago when record keeping at the arboretum was not as systematic as it is today, locating trees planted in memory of a family member or friend proved difficult. Sometimes, luck would save the day as it did when a woman showed up in search of a tree planted 20 years ago in memory of her son lost to SIDS (Sudden Infant Death Syndrome). She had never seen the tree and only had a card, signed by friends and co-workers, telling her that one had been planted in her son's memory. Jheri combed through the arboretum's database and came across a tree simply labeled "SIDS." It was an oak.

When the woman set out to see the tree, a young man accompanied her. "I never knew my brother," he told Jheri. He asked if he could take a leaf from the tree. He tugged at the oak leaf and tears ran down his face.

Surely one of the more remarkable living memorial trees is the one that has taken root at the site of the World Trade Center where 2,606 people died in the terrorist attacks on Sept. 11, 2001. It's hard to imagine a tree surviving the devastation wrought by the collapse of the Twin Towers, but somehow an 8-foot-tall Callery pear tree did. Recovery workers discovered the tree badly scorched by fire with only one living branch. Its future looked bleak at best.

Cared for at a nursery in the Bronx, the pear tree did something no one expected. It spurted back to life the next spring. The tree's survival seemed assured until March 2010, when a wild spring storm blew through the city and uprooted the pear tree. Would this finally bring an end to its miraculous life? Not a chance. Landscape experts replanted the tree and declared it unharmed.

Undaunted by storms and terrorist attacks, the Ground Zero Survivor Tree now stands 30 feet tall. Nearby, rising up to 1,776 feet, is the newly constructed One World Trade Center that has now become the tallest structure in the U.S. with the recent addition of a 408-foot spire at its pinnacle. Though a beacon on the spire will soon be seen miles away, don't expect the pear tree to be overlooked this upcoming Memorial Day when victims' families will remember those who perished on Sept. 11, 2001.

It doesn't matter if a memorial tree grows on hallowed ground in the heart of New York City or on a pedestal of dirt in the Yakima Area Arboretum. The pear tree and the dogwood speak to hope in a world far too crowded with darkness and despair.

# Military uncles form true appreciation of Memorial Day

*May 27, 2012*

Under a soot-gray blanket of clouds, snow fell in swirls, filling the thick forest along Belgium's Ardennes with ghostly white figures of ice. It was 5:30 a.m. on the morning of Dec. 16, 1944, the first day of what would be called the Battle of the Bulge, the largest and bloodiest battle that American forces would fight during World War II.

The German's 6th Panzer Army unleashed a 90-minute barrage using 1,600-military pieces. Trees exploded into splinters and chaos rained down upon the American troops.

Among those caught by the surprise attack was Lt. Tommy Sollitt. Tommy grew up in Chicago, the oldest of four children to George and Blanche Sollitt. He had gone to Purdue and played football. He studied engineering, hoping in time to take a prominent role in his father's construction company.

On that first day of the Battle of the Bulge, he and a military chaplain were walking along the battle lines and came upon a group of soldiers from his artillery company. The soldiers were trying to defuse a land mine. The 27-year-old lieutenant stopped to help. Just then the land mine exploded, sending lethal shards of metal in all directions. The lieutenant died instantly.

He was my Uncle Tommy, one of the 19,000 Americans killed in the Battle of the Bulge. I never met him and only knew what he looked like from weathered photographs. He was handsome and so young. He had a son who was born several months after his death. His name also was Tommy.

On the other side of the world, Bruce Lippincott had orders to patrol a river deep within China. He was a U.S. Navy officer and was practicing critical maneuvers his men would take if the Japanese military attacked.

My Uncle Bruce Lippincott.

It was a daunting task filled with uncertainties. Already, the Japanese had devastated the poorly led forces of China's National Revolutionary Army under the command of Chiang Kai-shek. From April to the end of December 1944, Japan's superior forces had wounded or killed 300,000 of the Chinese troops and had left more than 200,000 civilians dead.

War is always a calculation of risks and luck. The Japanese forces marched in a different direction and never ventured through the river region where the 23-year-old Navy officer stood ready to defend.

That officer was my uncle, too.

I had two wartime uncles with two different destinies, a life cut short and another saved.

Two years after the war ended, Bruce married Nancy Sollitt, the youngest of Uncle Tommy's three sisters. Marian, my mother, was the oldest.

After grandfather Sollitt died, Uncle Bruce helped to lead the Chicago construction company and, no doubt, would have worked alongside Uncle Tommy had he survived the war.

Uncle Bruce and Aunt Nancy raised three sons. Later they moved to Seattle, where my uncle set up a successful extension of Sollitt Construction.

They eventually moved to Whidbey Island, where Uncle Bruce could be surrounded by water. He loved boating, thanks to his father who was famous in the world of sailing, having developed a handicapping system that allowed sailboats of all sizes to start a race at the same time.

Uncle Bruce owned sleek-looking sailboats, cabin cruisers and even a tugboat, the Bee, which he kept at a slip in Lake Union. On one sunny day, he took his family and mine on a tour of Lake Washington, the mighty Bee chugging along at a modest 5-mph clip.

A gracious and decent man who fought for what he believed in and for his country as well, Uncle Bruce died May 10 at Providence Hospital in Everett. He was 91.

The story of my two uncles speaks to the remarkable sacrifices men and women in uniform have endured so others could fulfill their dreams. That's why Memorial Day is set aside to honor those who have died in service to this nation.

Its roots reach back to the Civil War when women in the South decorated the graves of Confederate soldiers. And there were many to decorate. On the bloodiest single-day battle in American history — Sept. 17, 1862, in the Battle of Antietam — more than 23,000 Union and Confederate soldiers were either killed or wounded.

Americans first celebrated Memorial Day on May 30, 1868. Decorating grave sites and displaying American flags became routine, as were parades and speeches.

That tradition, though, has faded over time. Few parades are held and flags now adorn T-shirts and automobile advertisements. Even the date fluctuates. Instead of May 30, Memorial Day falls on the last Monday of the month so we can enjoy a three-day holiday. We have eroded the meaning of Memorial Day by making it too convenient, too easy to forget. We just don't get it, do we? It's about time we take a hard look at what we have become as a nation — self-indulgent.

We feel entitled to our freedom, to our excesses. What about that young lieutenant who once bled for us nearly 70 years ago in the bitter cold of the Ardennes, thousands of miles from home?

It certainly wasn't convenient for my Uncle Tommy and Uncle Bruce to serve our country. But they did, and we are better for it. That I'm sure of.

# Best gifts for Mom won't be given today

*May 14, 2000*

E ggs Benedict in bed.

Far too many of us have reduced Mother's Day to this "sauce de resistance" — a thick, ochre-colored hollandaise that has way too many bad things in it to be of lasting value. Except for boosting mom's cholesterol count.

We have made Mother's Day too predictable. Flowers, a dinner out, cards from Hallmark are the norm, not the exception. There's no element of surprise, aside from the extravagance of the gifts or, heaven forbid, the pathetic excuse that you had somehow forgotten.

That's why my most memorable gifts to my mother had nothing to do with Mother's Day. Several stand out as the very best. It will be hard to top them for their magical brew of ingenuity and spontaneity, both of which are essential when gifts from the heart are extended to the one who bore you into this life with excruciating agony and greeted your shrill cries with a smile and a warm caress, who once stayed up for days on end as you, at age 5, suffered through pneumonia and watched the wallpaper slide off the walls as the vaporizer spewed out its therapeutic mist. She was always there, her voice and face a heartbeat away. Yes, you owe it to your mom to be at the top of your game when seeking out a gift.

One of those gifts, though, took a bit of money and a crash course on conversational Spanish. It happened years ago when I was in college in the late 1960s, at about the time anti-war demonstrations were taking hold and a few months after I began sporting a mustache that, to this day, my mother has never quite understood. "You still have that," she notes each time I visit our family home near Chicago.

So there I was in the '60s, wearing bell-bottom pants and thoroughly impoverished. My mom and dad had traveled that spring to Spain with some friends. The trip would span my mother's birthday. Because of this, my older brother and older sister had concluded they were off the hook for a birthday gift. I decided, though, something had to be done, something with a little pizzazz. But how do you get a gift delivered to someone who's halfway across the globe?

I was totally in the dark about where my parents were staying. They probably figured it wasn't wise to provide a college student with their itinerary. After about 10 or so phone calls to my mom's friends in Chicago, I located the place where she would be staying on her birthday. It turned out to be a dinky hotel in a little town a hundred or so miles from Madrid.

Undeterred by the geographical hurdles that lay before me, I approached a florist in Meadville, Pennsylvania, the small city where I was attending Allegheny College. It took a short, but passionate speech to finally convince the local florist to contact a floral shop outside Madrid. After a series of excruciating exchanges across the Atlantic Ocean and after clearing out my anemic bank account, the fix was in. Flowers were to be delivered at the hotel in one of Spain's smallest towns on my mother's birthday.

Though it took place more than 30 years ago, my mother still gets teary-eyed when talking about the time she stepped into a hotel in rural Spain to find, waiting for her on a table with dusty linen, a colorful bouquet of flowers from a son whom she thought had long ago forgotten her in the haste to grow up and be free.

My best surprise gift I gave to my mom didn't involve a birthday or any special occasion. I was 9 years old at the time and held to the firm belief that my mother was the greatest human being in the universe. So, in a moment of inspiration, I tucked my weekly allowance into the back pocket of my jeans and headed out in search of a gift befitting a person of such stature.

On a day that held no particular importance other than it was sunny and warm outside, I pedaled my bike to the local drugstore. My arrival was announced several blocks away for I had made the prudent move of clipping two playing cards with clothespins to the rear wheel of my bike. With the stiff cards slapping against the spokes of the wheel, I was able to produce, at least to my ears, the hypnotic clicking sound of a finely tuned engine.

Upon arriving at Huerbinger's Drug Store, I asked the clerk if I could take a look at their collection of earrings. Back then, drugstores sold everything, especially baseball cards of which I had purchased hundreds. But this time it was for Mom. I picked out a particularly splashy set of purple earrings and returned to my Schwinn, its silent motor ready to be revved up for action.

Astonishment greeted my return home, my hands outstretched with a gift that only a mother could cherish. I can't recall her wearing them much after that, but for a kid who still roamed the neighborhood with his Davy Crockett Daisy air rifle, the deed had been done, and besides, there were other hills to climb and gifts to ponder.

Years later, a thief broke into our family home and stole all of my mom's wedding silverware. Also swiped were a box of expensive jewelry and a set of purple earrings, which really shouldn't have been there if it hadn't been for a mother who cared enough to show her son it was all right to tell the world there's more to love in life than just yourself.

# Talking about how a life ends

*August 23, 2009*

Talk of death happens in hallways, from doctors in white smocks and late at night when there's no coffee and little hope for sleep.

I sat in the waiting room, alone, in an unfamiliar hospital trying to get my mind wrapped around what was unfolding. I had arrived only a few hours earlier, running between airport concourses on a series of flights from Yakima to the suburbs of Chicago.

"What's the end game here, Mr. Hatton?" the doctor asked as he leaned forward, his eyes focused on mine as a thin stream of tears slipped slowly down my face. It was around 1 a.m. and I was exhausted.

Several hours earlier, my mother had undergone emergency surgery. No one knew what was going on. She had collapsed in the entryway of her home. Medics had arrived and whisked her away in an ambulance.

When I arrived at the hospital, nurses were preparing to take her down to surgery. My mom was 88 and undergoing chemotherapy treatment for fourth-stage lung cancer. Her mind was sharp, but her physical health was failing.

X-rays had shown a suspicious area in her intestines. That's why a surgeon was being called in from Chicago.

The hospital staff made sure paperwork for the surgery was in order. She nodded her head when they asked again if she wanted the procedure.

This was two years ago, long before Sarah Palin had ever mentioned the phrase "death panels" and before talk show hosts had stirred up unfounded fears that a reformed health care system would "pull the plug on grandma." The hysteria began innocently enough with a provision that would allow Medicare to pay for end-of-life discussions with your doctor.

Few in this nation really talk about death. We know it's important, but seldom do we sit down with family members and doctors to discuss what treatment options should be considered in the final stages of life.

My sister Kathy, Mom and me in a photo taken on April 7, 2007. It was Mom's 88th birthday, just seven months before her death.

My mom did. She had an advance directive that broadly spelled out her wishes. On her medical chart were the bold letters DNR (do not resuscitate). In other words, if death tugged at her life, we were supposed to let go, to let death take hold.

Even with directives, though, there are twists and turns.

Downstairs in the surgical unit, I held my mom's hand and we waited. The place was empty. It was late on a Saturday afternoon. The surgeon finally appeared. I whispered in Mom's ear, "I love you," as nurses wheeled her away, her bed fading into the shadows of the surgical unit. The doors closed and I was left there alone.

Two hours later, the surgeon reappeared.

The operation had revealed a perforated intestine — one of the worst possible outcomes. If trauma from the surgery doesn't kill your mother, the surgeon told me, infection will. He said he didn't expect her to make it through the night.

I headed up to the Intensive Care Unit and found Mom breathing through a ventilator and surrounded by a tangle of pneumatic pumps and machines required for patients after surgery.

The ICU's attending physician repeated the question: "What's the end game?"

I had to make a decision. Her blood pressure was dropping. Should they go ahead and artificially increase it?

"That could be seen as aggressive care," the physician said, referring to Mom's directive against heroic measures.

I could have said no, and Mom would have presumably died within a few hours. But I also knew I wanted my sister there. She was flying in from New York state and would arrive the next morning.

So I told the physician to go ahead with the procedure. Mom made it through the night.

My sister Kathy joined me the next day and we kept vigil at Mom's bedside. Each day brought a new drama. Several times we were told she could pass away within the hour. But somehow she survived. She even defied the odds and breathed on her own when the ventilator was removed.

In a week, she was transferred to a regular hospital room. We even conferred with social workers about sending her to a nursing home to recover. But the infection in her abdomen kept returning.

Late one afternoon, a doctor pulled us aside in the hallway. He told us the antibiotics being fed intravenously were all that were keeping her alive. How long would she live without them? I asked.

Maybe 24 hours, he said. Maybe less.

Again, we faced the question: "What's the end game?" What did we hope to gain in these final hours of her life?

Both my sister and I knew that answer. Mom wanted to go home, to the place where she had lived the past five decades, where she had raised three children and entertained close friends during her life.

Hospice workers made that happen. When the ambulance driver asked her where she was going, she replied without hesitation, "I'm going home."

The next day, some 24 hours later, she died.

The doctors had been right, and so had we.

# Son's wedding latest of many happy memories

*September 15, 2013*

O n a road trip of great expectations, we drove past Butte, Montana, with its signature downtown attraction — the former Anaconda open pit copper mine. A few minutes later, we crested Homestake Pass marking the Continental Divide. Along this 6,329-foot spine of rocks and pine, water from passing storms flow east to the Atlantic Ocean or west to the Columbia River and the Pacific. It's nature's perfect watershed, separating rain, snow, sleet and morning dew in equal portions.

Watershed also describes a turning point in a person's life, and that's exactly what my wife, Leslie, and I were about to witness. My 33-year-old son Andy, and Leslie's stepson of eight years, was about to be married in Billings, where his bride, Leann, grew up.

Many watershed moments highlight a parent's life. Some are lighthearted like a child's first birthday party. Others are not, like the first time your son calls to tell you he was in an automobile accident. As a father, I always seemed ill prepared for when they occurred. You try to be ready, try to do the right thing or say the right words, but it rarely works out the way you had envisioned.

Let's take, for instance, the early morning hours of April 11, 1980, when my life's resume expanded to include the title "Dad."

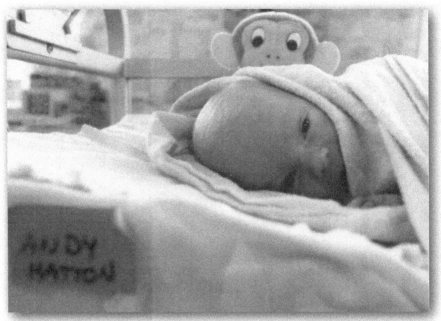

Andy and his stuffed monkey stare out into the hospital's preemie ward.

The setting was in the surgical unit at the University of Washington Medical Center. Andy arrived 10 weeks early and weighed a mere 3 pounds 2 ounces. He spent his first month in the neo-natal clinic with other pint-sized infants, some not even weighing two pounds. Always the optimist, I figured Andy would breeze through those early days with few complications. Such are the delusions of parenthood. All sorts of problems could have befallen him, from life-threatening infections to apnea where his breathing could stop temporarily.

These apnea episodes happened far too often. He was hooked up to several monitors. When he stopped breathing, bells would go off and a nurse would tap the outside of his portable incubator with her knuckles. That would jostle Andy back to breathing again. It's terrifying for a parent to see but Andy didn't seem to mind. His tiny arms would twitch wildly about and on he went, sucking in air and whistling it out through the small portals of his nose.

When I carried Andy out of the hospital and brought him home for the first time, that was momentous, too. On his first Sunday away from the hospital's noisy monitors, Andy received a different kind of wake-up call. It was the sound of our front door banging loudly from a mammoth sonic boom caused by the eruption of Mount St. Helens. Just what our family needed at the time, more drama.

Another turning point can also be as innocent as a child losing his or her first tooth. Again with Andy, nothing was simple. He was in first grade at the time. His mom had made him an egg salad sandwich for lunch. At about noon that day, I received a panicked call to head down to Nob Hill Elementary School. Andy was crying uncontrollably, his teacher told me. He had swallowed his tooth.

Again, parents are confronted almost daily with these comical but thorny turn of events. Being a good storyteller helps. We concocted an exotic tale about the Tooth Fairy having magical powers to divine the very moment when a tooth becomes dislodged. It worked. We then had Andy write a note that read, in part, "Dear Tooth Fairy: I owe you one tooth." He placed the note under his pillow that night. At 3 a.m., I did my best impression of a trained Navy Seal and crawled along the carpet to his room. I gently extracted the note from under his pillow and replaced it with a shiny silver dollar. Mission accomplished.

A son's first date is another milestone, but on a different scale. Nothing, though, prepared me for the girl standing on the other side of our front door. While it might not qualify as an official date, it was the first time Andy had a girl calling for him. Luckily, he had just left the house with several friends.

When I opened the door I couldn't help staring at the girl's nose. She had a ring in it. Her hair was dyed a sooty black and her lips were smeared in a moist, inky dark lipstick. The all-black outfit sealed the deal: She was a Goth, a post-punk rocker.

"Andy's not here," I said loudly when she asked about my son. I tried to leave the impression that he would never, ever return to our home. It must have worked. I never saw the Goth girl again.

Much has happened since those days when my son was a teenager. That thought raced through my mind as I sat down in the historic Billings Depot on a hot August afternoon and listened to Andy and Leann recite their wedding vows. Andy wrote the script, filled with flights of humor and pledges of commitment.

Leann and Andy, the newlyweds.

Later at the reception, I stood up to make a toast and looked across the room at Andy's aunts, uncles, cousins and friends who had traveled from South Carolina, New York, Connecticut, Boston, Chicago and Seattle to celebrate this moment. I knew, too, that there were two faces missing in the crowded room — the faces of Bonnie, his mother, and his younger brother, Jed. His mother died from cancer 13 years ago and his younger brother lost his life following complications from a seizure in the fall of 2002. Andy loved them dearly, as much as a son and brother could.

So I raised a toast in their honor and told Andy how proud they would have been of him on this day, this watershed moment filled with such hope and promise. I could tell by the tenderness in his eyes that his mom and brother would never be far from him.

I could also tell in his smile what this moment indeed meant. It was the same smile that greeted me when he first said "Dada" and reached out to me, his arms twitching wildly in the air.

# Afterword

*"The difficulty … is to say no more than we know."*
— Isaac Bashevis Singer, Nobel Prize
Laureate for Literature

# Donating to scholarship fund

Proceeds from the sale of "More To Crow About" will be donated to a scholarship fund in honor of my late wife, Bronnie, who died on Oct. 16, 2000, from ovarian cancer. The fund helps aspiring special education teachers at Central Washington University, where Bronnie earned her diploma.

If you wish to make a personal contribution to the scholarship fund, please write your check to: CWU Foundation - Bronwen Hatton Endowed Scholarship. Mail your contribution to:

Central Washington University Foundation
400 East University Way
Ellensburg, WA 98926-7508

And thanks for extending a helping hand to future special education teachers.

*Also by Spencer Hatton:*

## "Counting Crows: Stories of Love, Laughter and Loss"

---

What do basketball legend Wilt "The Stilt" Chamberlain, the Queen Mother of England, actor Al Pacino, writer Kurt Vonnegut, blues great B.B. King and Lady Bird Johnson have in common? They have crossed paths with Spencer Hatton during his nearly four decades as a journalist and award-winning columnist. These famous people are just a few of the colorful personalities found inside the pages of "Counting Crows: Stories of Love, Laughter and Loss."

Ever walk down the aisle at the Little White Wedding Chapel in Las Vegas holding onto the arm of an Elvis impersonator? The author has and describes in detail what happened during his hilarious marriage ceremony.

You will also get to meet a group of courageous fathers who, like the author, have raised children with special needs.

And then there are the long, painful steps the writer takes following the death of his wife, and two years later, the tragic death of his 18-year-old son, Jed. It's a journey of deep sorrow, fresh discoveries and renewed hope, making "Counting Crows" a reading experience not to be missed.

— Winner of two national book awards —
Finalist, Non-Fiction, 2013 Indie Excellence Book Awards
2013 Beach Book Festival

What readers say about "Counting Crows" on Amazon:

*Love this book! Counting Crows has already received acclaim and been cited for book awards. Treat yourself and your friends to this very special gift. The author brings to the table a smorgasbord of life experiences in very short stories. His training as a U.S. army medic served him well as he and his wife faced two huge challenges: her long brave battle against ovarian cancer, and the diagnosis of autism for their younger son. Yet this is a very balanced account of their lives ranging from anguishing times to hilarious ones. Men and women, young or old will be captivated by these great stories.*

— M. K. MOORE

*I just bought Mr. Hatton's book and I find it to be touching, humorous and poignant. The author is very honest and isn't afraid to share some of his deepest losses and his feelings surrounding these losses. Mr. Hatton has a wonderful sense of humor that often shows up in his book, sometimes, when least expected. I feel privileged to be from the same town as the author and have enjoyed his weekly newspapers columns for years so I was very excited to purchase his book. I also bought books for two friends that live back east.*

— KATHI H.

*Love this book. Purchased a few more copies for friends. While already a fan of Mr. Hatton's writings, I am now an even more devoted fan. Many parts of this book will stay with me forever. Who knows what makes a writer so readable, but whatever it is Mr. Hatton has it in spades. Many thanks to the author for sharing his journey (so far) and I sincerely hope he gives us more.*

— MS. READS-A-LOT

*Spencer writes from the heart with compassion and humor, telling it like it is in real-life situations he's experienced first hand. You WILL laugh and cry as you read these very personal accountings from his life.*

— CYNTHIA M.

*Spencer Hatton has hit a "home run" with his first book, "Counting Crows." He writes as if he is talking to the reader and that is what makes it so enjoyable. He can make you laugh and make you cry within the span of only a few pages. Now that is real talent! I am looking forward to his next book with great anticipation.*

— PAUL R.

From a posting on Facebook

*I'm highly recommending this book. Not just because as a friend, I am blessed to be featured in it. It's full of Spencer's articles over many years at the Yakima Herald-Republic. He is a prolific writer who will have you laughing, smiling, grinning and yes, even sobbing. Wait. Doesn't the Readers Digest do that too? What a star! Congrats and great success my friend.*

— DALE CARPENTER

(Dale died in December 2013 from cancer. He was featured in "Counting Crows: Stories of Love, Laughter and Loss")